Adolescent Suicide

WILEY SERIES ON PSYCHOLOGICAL DISORDERS

IRVING B. WEINER, *Editor*
The University of Rochester Medical Center

Adolescent Suicide

Jerry Jacobs

WILEY-INTERSCIENCE   A Division of John Wiley & Sons, Inc.
New York • London • Sydney • Toronto

Library of Congress Catalogue Card Number: 78–149773
ISBN 0–471–43590–2

Printed in the United States of America.

10 9 8 7 6 5 4 3 2 1

To all of those whose personal circumstances exact from them an heroic effort to "just stay alive."

Series Preface

This series of books is addressed to behavioral scientists concerned with understanding and ameliorating psychological disorders. Its scope should prove pertinent to clinicians and their students in psychology, psychiatry, social work, and other disciplines that deal with problems of human behavior as well as to theoreticians and researchers studying these problems. Although many facets of behavioral science have relevance to psychological disorder, the series concentrates on the three core clinical areas of psychopathology, personality assessment, and psychotherapy.

Each of these clinical areas can be discussed in terms of theoretical foundations that identify directions for further development, empirical data that summarize current knowledge, and practical applications that guide the clinician in his work with patients. The books in this series present scholarly integrations of such theoretical empirical, and practical approaches to clinical concerns. Some pursue the implications of research findings for the validity of alternative theoretical frameworks or for the utility of various modes of clinical practice; others consider the implications of certain conceptual models for lines of research or for the elaboration of clinical methods; and others encompass a wide range of theoretical, research, and practical issues as they pertain to a specific psychological disturbance, assessment technique, or treatment modality.

University of Rochester   IRVING B. WEINER
Rochester, New York

Preface

This book was written to give the reader a better understanding of how an individual comes to believe that suicide is "the only way out." The perspective adopted throughout the work is that of the actor. The book is concerned with the personal situations of suicides and suicide attempters and how these situations ultimately led to the victim experiencing an end of hope.

While there is a considerable psychiatric literature concerned with the personal situations of suicides and suicide attempters, these works almost always "interpret" the suicide's circumstances within a psychoanalytic framework, or otherwise superimpose upon the data some external and synthetic system of analysis, the better to "make sense" of an otherwise seemingly irrational form of behavior. Contrary to the above approach, the author has taken the suicides' accounts at face value and analyzed them within a frame of reference which renders these accounts reasonable not "even when" but "especially when" they are taken seriously.

I have referred above to the psychiatric literature concerned with the personal situations of suicides and suicide attempters. What of the sociological literature? Durkheim's profound influence upon the sociological study of suicide and other social phenomena has led sociologists to adopt a different methodological approach. Sociologists concerned with the individual, his intentions, motives, or morals, have long been considered by their colleagues to be guilty of "psychologizing" or "philosophizing." As a result, the psychiatric and/or sociological literature is practically nonexistent that deals with the individual's intentions, motives and morals as presented by him and accepted "as is" by the researcher for analysis. Nor are the events that constitute the suicide's personal circumstances systematically considered, either with or without a control group. In those rare instances where they are considered at all, they are generally held to have no relationship to suicide or suicide attempts.

This work was undertaken to help rectify this serious gap in the existing literature which has resulted from the prevalence and persistence of traditional psychiatric and sociological explanations of suicide. It is also held that suicides and suicide attempters have too long and too often been misunderstood and misjudged. I refer here to the notion that suicide is some-how pathological, sinful, and/or immoral. Such contentions are generally based upon the neglect of any serious consideration of the suicide's personal situations over time and his persistent struggle to overcome them and survive. Finally, I have attempted to present some suggestions as to what can be done to help prevent suicide and why existing programs are not promis-ing in this regard.

The book is divided into four chapters: Theories of Suicide, Theoretical-Methodological Orientation, Findings and Interpretation of Data, and Conclusions and Implications for Suicide Prevention. The chapter headings are self-explanatory. The data and its analysis offer at least a partial answer to the critical question . . . what was it that the individual experienced that led him to believe that suicide was "the only way out," and having reached that point, how was he able to act upon it and take his own life?

Finally, I would like to thank those persons who assisted with, or were otherwise helpful in the course of this study. First let me thank Professor Richard T. Morris of U.C.L.A. for his many helpful suggestions and the understanding guidance he offered during the preparation of an earlier draft of the manuscript. Thanks, too, to Miss Donna Katz, my research assistant, for so ably assisting with the interviewing of the suicide attempt-ters and their parents, in the writing of the case histories, and in the drawing up of the life history charts. Her display of incentive and integrity in the above regard were, I believe, extraordinary. Finally, thanks to Alan Bomser, now with California State College, Dominguez Hills, for a job well done in supervising the home interviews of the control adolescents and their parents.

While I am indebted to all of the above, I accept the sole responsibility for the work which follows.

JERRY JACOBS

April, 1971

Contents

ix

x   **Contents**

List of Tables

PGS
1 STATISTICS
REASON — TRAD

CHAPTER 1

Theories of Suicide

Suicide is the fifth leading cause of death among adolescents in the 15 to 19 year-old age group. It is exceeded only by accidents, malignant neoplasms, cardiovascular-renal disease, and homocides. Suicide rates for adolescents, age 15 to 19, increased 67% between 1954 and 1964. Estimates of the number of suicide attempts to suicides among adolescents range from 7 to 50.[1]

The traditional explanation of these statistics by those most often asked to explain, anticipate and prevent suicide, is that adolescent suicide and suicide attempts result from some form of unconscious, irrational, maladaptive, or impulsive act. These four basic underlying assumptions are incorporated into most psychological explanations of suicide and suicide attempts. Psychiatrists, clinical psychologists, social workers and some less positivistic sociologists all adhere to them.

I believe that these assumptions are unwarranted and difficult to maintain in the light of the evidence. From a phenomenological perspective which takes seriously the accounts of adolescent suicides and suicide attempters, one can only conclude that suicide and suicide attempts result from a conscious rational choice. Indeed, it is difficult to imagine a definition of suicide that does not acknowledge intentionality. The general exclusion of intentionality from previous theories of suicide is no accident. Attempts at explaining suicide as a conscious, rational act have thus far been eminently unsuccessful.

If psychological explanations of suicide have been of little assistance in understanding, anticipating or preventing suicide, the traditional sociological perspective on suicide proposed by Durkheim has done little to rectify this shortcoming. An explanation of suicide rates based upon the notion of a relative lack of social integration is of no assistance whatever in explaining, anticipating or preventing the suicide of any particular person. To the extent that one is interested in understanding suicides, a review and revision of the above explanations and the various theories incorporating them is essential. The author will undertake such a revision in this work. A new perspective will be offered from which to view suicide . . . the one adopted by the suicide himself.

Notwithstanding the desirability of achieving this perspective (without first becoming suicidal), all existing explanations of suicide have systematically avoided it. The reasons for this neglect and a means of overcoming it will be presented in the following pages.

DURKHEIM AND THE "ETIOLOGICAL" APPROACH

Durkheim set about establishing the superiority of the "aetological" over the "morphological" approach by attempting to systematically discredit the latter. A description of the morphological approach and the problems Durkheim felt were inherent in pursuing it, are given as follows:

> . . . it would seem to be best to inquire first whether the tendency [to suicide] is single and indestructible or whether it does not rather consist of several different tendencies. . . . If so, we should . . . . observe and describe as many [cases] as possible. . . . If all were found to have the same essential characteristics, they should be grouped in a single class; otherwise, . . . a certain number of species should be determined according to their resemblances and differences. One would admit as many suicidal currents as there were distinct types, then seek to determine their causes and respective importance. *We have pursued some such method in our brief study of the suicide of insanity.*
>
> *Unfortunately, no classification of the suicides of sane persons can be made in terms of their morphological types or characteristics, from almost complete lack of the necessary data. To be attempted, it would require good descriptions of many individual cases. One would have to know the psychological condition of the suicide at the moment of forming his resolve, how he prepared to accomplish it, how he finally performed it, whether he were agitated or depressed, calm or exalted, anxious or irritated, etc. Now we have such data practically only for some cases of insane suicide. . . . We have almost no such information for others.*
> [Emphasis added]

For those few cases of normal suicide then available, Durkheim felt that the summaries were too brief and that:

> . . . the patient's revelations of his condition are usually insufficient, if not suspect. . . . Furthermore in view of the manner of execution of most suicides, proper observations are next to impossible.[2]

Having recognized that the classification of different categories of suicide based upon "good descriptions of many individual cases" was possible for suicides among the insane, he somehow felt it would be impossible to study sane people by the same approach. With the convenient disposal of the morphological approach and the search for the "essential characteristics" of suicide, Durkheim was free to substitute instead a system of explanation that sought its "causes." The methodology of the etiological approach is outlined as follows:

> But our aim may be achieved by another method. Let us reverse the order of study. . . . *we shall be able to determine the social types of suicide by classifying them not directly by their preliminarily described characteristics, but by the causes which produce them. Without asking why they differ from one another, we will first seek the social conditions responsible for them;* then group these conditions in a number of separate classes by their resemblances and differences, and we shall be sure that a specific type of suicide will correspond to each of these classes. *In a word, instead of being morphological, our classification will from the start be aetiological. Nor is this a sign of inferiority, for the nature of a phenomenon is much more profoundly got at by knowing its cause than by knowing its characteristics only, even the essential ones.*[3] [Emphasis added]

There was, of course, the recognized problem of seeking the causes to suicide when its characteristics, let alone its "essential characteristics," remained unknown. How would one know for what one had found the cause, when the characteristics of the phenomena under study were so nebulous? The dismissal of this objection and the basis for the remainder of Durkheim's book rests upon the fact that it was *a study of the social suicide rates, and not a study of suicide.*

> *The defect of this method, of course, is to assume the diversity of types without being able to identify them. It may prove their existence and number but not their special characteristics.* But this drawback may be obviated, at least in a certain measure. Once the nature of the causes is known we shall try to deduce the nature of the effects, since they will be both qualified and classified by their attachment to their respective sources. Of course, if this deduction were not at all guided by facts, it might be lost in purely imaginary constructions. . . . Alone, these data are too incomplete and unsure to provide a principle of classification; but once the outlines of this classification are found the data may be used.[4] [Emphasis added]

To be sure that the reader is clear on this point, Durkheim reminds him again . . . "we must not forget that what we are studying is the social-suicide-rate." [5]

Durkheim's decision to study social *suicide-rates* instead of *suicide* seems to be based upon the fact that the data for the former were plentiful and ready at hand, whereas a study of suicide was less convenient since the classification of suicide among sane persons would have required good descriptions of a great number of individual cases which were not then (or now) readily available. The use of an existing classification for insane persons according to morphological types was apparently acceptable since this was readily available. This about-face on the proper methodology of sociology is especially unsettling in light of the fact that Durkheim, in marshalling his argument against the relationship between suicide and insanity earlier in the book, assures us that:

> *The only methodical procedure consists of classifying according to their essential characteristics the suicides committed by insane persons, thus forming the principle types of insane suicide, and then trying to learn whether all cases of voluntary death can be included under these systematically arranged groups.*[6] [Emphasis added]

Durkheim abandoned this "only methodical procedure" for establishing differences in the essential characteristics of suicide and other phenomena, in order to establish his explanation of "causes" via the etiological approach.

Based on Durkheim's success with *Suicide* in discrediting psychological explanations and legitimizing sociological ones, nearly all future sociological studies of suicide, particularly in America, followed in his footsteps—Gibbs and Martin,[7] Henry and Short,[8] and Powell[9] all have in common the fact that their theories rest basically on an analysis of official suicide rates. The theories consist essentially of an explanation of these official rates by imputing meaning to the correlations which are found to exist between the rates and certain social conditions. *None of these studies is based upon the behavior of suicidal persons, their beliefs or their writings.*

However, there are differences within them. Some incorporate explanations of psychological phenomena to help explain the rates of suicide, while others are based exclusively on social phenomena. Henry and Short represent the former posture, whereas Gibbs and Martin have attempted to represent the latter. It is interesting to consider briefly some of the assumptions of these two positions and where Durkheim stands in relation to them. Considering Durkheim's position first, we note the great care he took in defining suicide in order to be able to treat the subject "scientifically."

A scientific investigation can thus be achieved only if it deals with comparable facts, ...

Our first task then must be to determine the order of facts to be studied under the name of suicides. Accordingly, we must inquire whether, among the different varieties of death, some have common qualities objective enough to be recognizable by all honest observers, specific enough not to be found elsewhere and also sufficiently kin to those commonly called suicides for us to retain the same term without breaking with common usage. . . . The essential thing is not to express with some precision what the average intelligence terms suicide, but to establish a category of objects permitting this classification, which are objectively established, that is, correspond to a definite aspect of things.[10]

In short, in order to proceed with the "scientific" study of suicide it was first necessary to carefully define it and having done so, deal only with those cases the definition allowed for. Durkheim's definition of suicide was based on conscious intentionality.

The common quality of all these possible forms of supreme renunciation is that the determining act is performed advisedly; that at the moment of acting the victim knows the certain result of his conduct, no matter what reason may have led him to act thus . . . .

We may then say conclusively: the term suicide is applied to all cases of death resulting directly or indirectly from a positive or negative act of the victim himself, *which he knows will produce this result.*[11] [Emphasis added.]

Excluded from this definition are all other acts "in which the victim is either not the author of his own end or else only its unconscious author." [12]

It should be clear from the above that Durkheim's initial emphasis in deriving his definition of suicide was based upon psychological considerations, i.e. intentionality. Equally clear is the way in which he completely ignored this basic construction in the remainder of his book. At no point does he seek to establish the intentionality of any of the persons comprising his official rates nor has he any way of knowing how many of those persons representing the official rates were sane or insane, or among the sane, how many were suicides. Certainly it is clear that the officials responsible for determining the causes of death, and compiling the statistics on which Durkheim's work was based, were not referring to his definition when making their designations.

Douglas cites five other key problems Durkheim and others faced in using official suicide rates as a basis of analysis.

> (1) Unreliability resulting from the choice of the official statistics to be used in making the tests of the sociological theories; (2) unreliability resulting from sub-cultural differences in the attempts to hide suicide; (3) unreliability resulting from the effects of different degrees of social integration on the official statistics keeping; (4) unreliability resulting from significant variations in the social imputation of motives; (5) unreliability resulting from better collection of statistics among certain populations.[13]

I believe it was no accident that Durkheim ignored his original definition of suicide and attempted to exclude all psychological factors from his theory. The etiological approach does not lend itself easily to the incorporation of psychological variables since these must be established morphologically, through detailed case studies.

MODERN DAY FOLLOWERS

The work of Henry and Short is a contemporary example of Durkheim's approach to the study of suicide. However, they too were unsuccessful in reconciling psychological explanations of suicide with the "aetological" approach. Their explanation of suicide rates is based primarily on a frustration-aggression model. It is presumed that suicide and homicide emanate from the same source, "extreme forms of aggression"[14] stemming from frustration. It is suggested that aggression turned inward will result in suicide, whereas aggression turned outward leads to murder. This is a difficult position to maintain. For example, Tuckman *et al.*,[15] in analyzing the emotional content of 165 suicide notes, find that in only one per cent was hostility directed inward. D. J. West found that one-third of all the murders committed in England and Wales were murder-suicides.[16] What's more, the suicides took place, in most cases, immediately following the murder. Here we have aggression turned outward and then inward by the same person within moments.

Another interesting finding of West's with respect to Henry and Short was ". . . that many of these murder-suicide cases provided another indication that many of these murder-suicide offenders were actuated by feelings of despair more than hostility."[17] It was also found that, "In the sample of ordinary murders, the incidence of previous suicidal attempts was as high as in samples of persons who have committed suicide."[18]

In his summary West states:

Unlike the murderers, who include an excess of young, unmarried males, and of individuals of the lowest social class, the murder-suicide offenders were in these respects more representative of the general community, and the majority of them were married and living in a conventional family setting free from criminal associations.[19]

An analysis of his data led West to conclude that half of the murder-suicides in his study were "sane" and free from any signs of mental illness. He went on to note that Wolfgang and Cavan went even further to say that murder followed by suicide is rarely committed by insane persons.[20]

The use of a frustration-aggression model to explain suicide or suicide rates is not peculiar to sociologists. It is most popular with psychiatrists and psychologists, and is often cited in the psychological literature. An example of a case history study utilizing this assumption for an analysis of its data is James Jan-Tausch's study of suicides among school children. Having compiled 41 case histories of children who suicided in the New Jersey public schools between 1960–63, he tells us,

The would-be suicide may get temporary relief from overt aggressive acts or he may have such strong feelings against persons close to him that he accepts guilt for harboring thoughts of violence and suppresses his true feelings. When this hostility is fully expressed it usually results in homicide or suicide.[21]

The frustration-aggression model does not adequately account for these contradictory findings. One way to contend with the problem of integrating psychological explanations into the methodology of the etiological approach is not to attempt it. This was the tack of Gibbs and Martin, who were actually more "sociological" in their explanation of suicide rates than Durkheim. This is not to say that they were more successful, eloquent, or insightful; they were not.

Gibbs and Martin were perceptive enough to recognize that although Durkheim's theory of suicide rates rested upon the proposition that there exists an inverse relationship between social integration and the suicide rate, ". . . at no point in Durkheim's monograph is there an explicit connotative definition of social integration, much less an operational definition." [22] It was to rectify this shortcoming that "A Theory of Status Integration and Its Relationship to Suicide" was written. Gibbs and Martin attempted to relate the degree of social integration to the stability and durability of social relationships. Unfortunately, there seemed no way to measure this either, so it was decided to "utilize observable conditions that presumably reflect these characteristics." [23] The "observable conditions" decided upon were the relative degree of role conflict to be inferred from the degree of status conflict to which various groups are subject. The measure of status integration (lack of status conflict) would be discovered by seeing "under what conditions will a large proportion of a population simultaneously occupy incompatible status?" ". . . In more specific terms, it assumed that the actual occupancy of statuses in a society reflects the degree of compatibility among statuses." [24] This, of course, assumes that everyone has equal access to available statuses and that if they are not found occupying them, it is because they have tried and left, having found them incompatible with other statuses they held. ". . . The person occupying two incompatible statuses will give up one or both because of dissatisfaction arising from attempts to conform to conflicting roles." [25] The logical extension of such a position might lead one to explain the status of Negroes as follows: Negroes occupying the positions of boot blacks and "custodians" are not found to also occupy the status of banker or lawyer, since these necessitate role conflict; the Negro, having occupied the status of Bank President, abandons it in favor of boot black, or he may, of course, abandon "both" statuses, which would be helpful in accounting for the high rates of unemployment among Negroes.

To these and other obvious intra-system dilemmas, Gibbs and Martin caution us not to throw the baby out with the bath water. After all, the proof is in the pudding, and the real question is, does it work? Powell, in testing the theory in Tulsa,[26] found that it did not work. For example, the "Professional-Managerial" category with the highest status integration measure should have the lowest suicide rate. Actually, five out of the remaining eight categories have lower suicide rates. Rank 8 (next to the lowest in status integration), the "Service" category, had next to the lowest instead of next to the highest suicide rate, etc. Does this convince Gibbs and Martin that there are serious shortcomings to their theory? Not really. After all, some of the nine status integration ranks correspond to the proper suicide rank, and if we presume these are correct and revise those categories with the contradictory correlations, we still stand a good chance of "empirically" demonstrating the validity of the theory, all evidence to the contrary notwithstanding.

Following in the footsteps of the etiological approach, with or without a psychological element, studies of suicide rates in various cities reveal the following: the upper class with the highest rates,[27] the lower class with the highest rates,[28] the upper and lower class with the highest rates and the middle class with the lowest rates,[29] and the middle class with the highest rates.[30]

It should be clear from all of this that in spite of Durkheim's brilliance in establishing sociology as a discipline in its own right, and notwithstanding his insight and eloquence, we ought to have some reservation about studying suicide or other social phenomena primarily from an etiological perspective based on an analysis of official statistical rates. In spite of Durkheim's contentions to the contrary, it might prove a very rewarding experience for sociologists to reevaluate the status of the morphological approach. The reason for sociology's reluctance to adapt the morphological approach is based upon several common sense assumptions made by Durkheim and his success in developing them. For example, Durkheim believed it extremely unlikely that one would find a common denominator in the personal situations of suicides.

> . . . the circumstances are almost infinite in number which are supposed to cause suicide. . . . This suggests that none of them is the specific cause. Could we perhaps at least describe causality to those qualities known to be common to all? But are there any such? . . . We see some men resist horrible misfortune, while others kill themselves after slight troubles. Moreover, we have shown that those who suffer most are not those who kill themselves most. Rather it is too great comfort which turns a man against himself. Life is most readily renounced at the time and among the classes where it is least harsh. At least, if it really sometimes occurs that the victim's personal situation is the effective cause of his resolve, such cases are very rare indeed and accordingly cannot explain the social suicide-rate.[31]

Unfortunately, Durkheim abandoned the search for those "qualities known to be common to all" before having begun it. Worse still is the fact that sociologists have since followed in his footsteps. Never having studied a number of specific cases of suicide in detail, how could Durkheim know that "some resist horrible misfortune, while others kill themselves after slight troubles," or that "those who suffer most are not those who kill themselves most," and lastly and most importantly, that "if it really sometimes occurs that the victim's personal situation is the effective cause of his resolve (to commit suicide), such cases are very rare indeed and accordingly cannot explain the social suicide-rate." [32] The author feels that such common sense assumptions are both unwarranted and misleading.

There is no need to assume the effects of one's personal situation on suicide. We need only refer to the suicide's own account for an accurate assessment.

> The comparison with imprisonment is no play on words. I am in prison, caught in a net from which I cannot free myself. I am a prisoner within myself; I get more and more tangled and every day is a new, useless struggle; the mesh is tightened more and

more. I am in Siberia; my heart is icebound, all around me is soli-
tude and cold. My best days are a sadly comic attempt to deceive
myself as to my true condition. It is undignified to live on like
this.[33]

It is clear from such accounts (when we take them seriously) that people
do not in fact kill themselves arbitrarily or impulsively.

PSYCHIATRIC EXPLANATIONS OF SUICIDE

What of those persons who do deal with personal situations in seeking
an explanation of suicide? What is their outlook? Durkheim notes:

Accordingly, even those who have ascribed most influence to individual conditions have sought these conditions less in such external incidents than in the intrinsic nature of the person, that is,
his biological constitution and the physical concomitants on which
it depends.[34]

This has been the general approach of psychiatrists, psychologists and
some less positivistic sociologists. The reason for this is that even among
those dealing with personal situations in case histories,[35] or with accounts
found in suicide notes, there seemed to be no common denominator to
suicide.

The inability of previous investigators to find a common denominator
necessary to explain suicide as resulting from a conscious rational process
has led them to conclude the necessity of in some way inferring the "real"
meaning of the suicide's story, either by superimposing upon the data an
unconscious irrational explanation or some other such synthetic system.

Conscious motives alone cannot adequately explain suicidal acts
because only certain people react in this manner to emotional
stress. With very few exceptions, there is no situation causing
individuals to commit suicide which would not be tolerated by
most other people without the emergence of self-destructive im-
pulses. People who tend to react to stressful situations with suicidal acts are called suicide prone.[36]

Most psychiatrists tend to interpret the accounts of their patients from this
general perspective. Here the emphasis is on the unconscious, impulsive
and/or irrational elements, the apparent rational aspects notwithstanding.

. . . It seemed that the most important motive for the suicide was
a need for punishment. The patient had been attempting to
escape his anger towards his mother for some years; finally, this

escape was no longer possible, and it was necessary for him to see that he was angry toward her. He was unable to tolerate this feeling and attempted to deal with it by running away, this time taking a trip to Mexico; yet this was not successful, and finally *he felt hopeless, as if he were left all alone. At this point he made his suicidal attempt.* It would seem that what was *really operative* here was an attempt to get back into the good graces of his mother by 'castrating' himself (by attempting to kill himself), and in this way to expiate his guilt. (Emphasis added.) [37]

One cannot help but wonder if perhaps it was not the fact that he felt hopeless and alone, (more than his attempt to get back into the good graces of his mother by castrating himself as a way to expiate his guilt) that led to his attempting suicide.

Stengel and Cook, in a discussion of the psychiatric approach to suicide, comment as follows on the above perspective.

> The problem of the mental state in which suicidal acts are carried out, irrespective of the presence of a mental illness, has long been controversial. Ever since Esquirol many physicians have held the opinion that the act of suicide alone is sufficient evidence of mental disorder. Henderson (1935) reaffirmed this view, and more recently Lindemann (1950) proposed to define suicide as a disease demanding epidemiological analysis. He coined the term "hypereridism" for "morbid states of hostile tension leading to suicide." [38]

The problem of proceeding on the above assumption is well put by C. Wright Mills:

> The quest for "real motives" set over against "mere rationalization" is often informed by a metaphysical view that the "real" motives are in some way biological. Accompanying such quests for something more real and back of rationalization is the view held by many sociologists that language is an external manifestation or concomitant of something prior, more genuine, and "deep" in the individual. "Real attitudes" versus "mere verbalization" or "opinion" implies that at best we only infer from his language what "really" is the individual's attitude or motive.
>
> Now what *could we possibly* so infer? Of precisely *what is* verbalization symptomatic? We cannot infer physiological processes from lingual phenomena. All we can infer and empirically check is another verbalization of the agent's which we believe was orienting and controlling behavior at the time the act was

performed. The only social items that can "lie deeper" are other lingual forms. The "Real Attitude or Motive" is not something different in kind from the verbalization of the "opinion." They turn out to be only relatively and temporally different.[39]

The author feels that in order to overcome this telling criticism, it is necessary to offer an explanation of suicide which is both derived from and validated by some empirical referent. I feel that the life situation of suicides, as related by them in case histories, diaries and in suicide notes, offers such a potential. I will seek to establish the common denominator of suicide in the formal aspects of a process to which suicidal persons were subject, rather than in some independent event such as a childhood trauma or a later "precipitating cause." It was the apparent lack of success in isolating a motive for suicide in some independent event of which Durkheim spoke. Analysts concerned with personal situations, whether they interpret them psychologically or not, often still proceed in this manner to seek the "aetiology" of suicide.

Since psychiatrists are the primary source of such case history material and their preoccupation is with the unconscious irrational components, how many of these researchers are concerned with viewing as a process the social-structural components of the life situations of suicides? Kahne, in reviewing the medical literature with respect to the paucity of studies dealing with the life situations of suicides, notes:

> There are occasional, marginal references to the importance of certain aspects of milieu organization as it might relate to patient suicide. On the whole, however, medical literature characteristically leaves the social arrangements and environmental conditions unintegrated with its general explanations of human suicide.[40]

If there has been a relative neglect of particular social-structural referents, there has been a complete neglect of these viewed as a process over time. The one exception to this I have found in the medical literature is Adolf Meyer.

Theodore Lidz, writing on Meyer, sums up his approach as follows:

> The meaning of Meyer's common sense psychiatry has often been misunderstood. He was not advocating that psychiatrists rely upon naive common sense: he devoted much of his life to teaching the uncommon sense provided by training and experience. *What he meant was that psychiatrists must be willing to use data about a patient's life in its own terms, not persist in seeking something behind and beyond the experience. . . .* He insisted

that the patient's life experiences were pertinent to etiology and provided guides to treatment, and that interest in the physiological must fit into study of the total pattern of a person's current behavior and its biographical origins . . . .[41] [Emphasis added]

An individual's behavior was learned behavior based upon experiences, and milieu manipulation was seen as very much a part of any plan for treatment. Meyer ". . . scrutinized life stories for what seemed to make the difference and search out common developmental factors in patients with similar difficulties." Lidz concluded his commemoration article on Meyer with this appeal to modern American psychiatry:

> He was a man of wisdom and perspective. I have tried to indicate that we still have a need for conscious awareness of his basic contributions. In commemorating him, we can do much for ourselves and for psychiatry by recognizing and utilizing the heritage he left us.[42]

If the existing literature is any indication of psychiatry's compliance with this recommendation, Lidz's appeal has fallen on deaf ears.

Although there exists a considerable psychiatric literature with regard to the case histories of suicides and suicide attempters, very few of these case histories are detailed enough to be useful in gaining an accurate assessment of the individual's "total biography." We have divided the literature into two basic sectors, those with detailed case histories covering extended periods of time, and those dealing superficially with life situations or dealing only with brief periods of time, and we have compiled the following samples.

Superficial Case Histories

Stengel and Cook (1958) include in their monograph thirty-one case histories of adult suicide attempters in London. The suicide attempters were interviewed by a doctor at the hospital where all were initially seen. The relatives were interviewed by a psychiatric social worker (Cook). In addition to the initial interview, there was a follow-up study in order to "ascertain the patients' state of health and the immediate and long term effects of the suicidal attempt on the relationship to their environments." [43] An interesting finding was that many of the suicide attempters succeeded in altering their personal circumstances to their advantage so that further attempts at suicide did not become defined is necessary. My own experience with primarily lower class adolescent suicide attempters indicates that the suicide attempt either leaves things essentially unchanged or more often than not adds to the adolescent's problems.[44]

The following is an example of a "superficial" case history taken from the thirty-one cases cited by Stengel and Cook. However, it is not typical of those generally given in the psychiatric literature, in that it offers a better description of the social environment than most.

> Case 22: Mrs. A. Y., born 1910, had been intermittently depressed for nearly five years since the loss of a premature baby, for which she blamed the hospital. She relapsed again on learning that a neighbor was pregnant. She tried to kill herself and her only child by barbiturates and coal gas. In hospital she presented severe depressive symptoms with marked hysterical features. Matrimonial difficulties concerned with her husband's suspected unfaithfulness played a part in the etiology of her illness. Her husband, for professional reasons, was away from home a great deal, and the patient had been living with two elder sisters, one of whom was an aggressive psychopath who dominated her. She saw her husband only at weekends. She had been unable to make up her mind to join him, had been living in constant conflict of loyalties, and had remained dependent on her family. On discharge from hospital she decided to leave her sisters and set up home at her husband's place of work away from her family. He had become more tolerant of her, and their relationship showed a distinct improvement in that they made mutual concessions. Five years after her suicidal attempt new difficulties arose, but no further suicidal attempt had occurred.
>
> The suicidal attempt brought about the patient's admission to hospital and treatment after she had suffered from severe depression for a very considerable period. Her overdependence on her family ceased and was replaced by a more mature relationship. Her relationship to her husband improved. Even more so than before the attempt, she concentrated her affection, a possessive overanxiety, on her child, who reciprocated by acting as her defender against the father.[45]

The richness of the above account is perhaps best appreciated in contrast to other accounts. For example, Stearns (1953) gives the case histories of twenty-five boys, ages 11–16, who died by hanging themselves in Massachusetts. There is a case history for each, about a paragraph long, from which Stearns concluded that there was no apparent reason for the suicide. He feels that in all cases the act took place abruptly in the midst of what seemed a well adjusted life. However, in some instances all of the clothes were removed and in others the boy was found hanging by the neck in girl's clothing. Case Number 2 is typical of those in this series.

> Age 14. Slow in school; disliked school and had threatened to run away. He had been on probation for petty stealing. Was

found hanging in the cellar of his home at 11:03 A.M., fully clad.[46]

Cavan (1928) lists fifty-five cases of suicide and murder-suicide, most of which are brief and superficial. There are two exceptions, cases XXIX and XXX, both of which are diaries. Case I also offers a fair amount of detail.[47] Cavan's work, although it is not a part of the psychiatric literature on suicide, is included for two reasons—first, because it is an exception to sociology's general abhorrence of the case history approach, and secondly, because her interpretation of why the murder-suicide occurred (e.g. in case XXIX) is basically psychological.

D. J. West offers a series of case histories of murder-suicides in his monograph, *Murder Followed by Suicide* (1965).[48] Only a representative sample of the 148 cases studied are present in his work. These were compared with the case histories of 148 murders. The case histories offer many interesting findings which (notwithstanding West's intent) can be used to question many traditional psychological and psychiatric explanations of suicide or murder-suicide offered so freely in the literature. Some of these aspects have been noted earlier in the chapter.

Greenwald and his assistants (1958) interviewed twenty prostitutes, fifteen of whom had made one or more suicide attempts. Brief case history summaries are included in the appendix.[49]

Robins *et al.,* in an article entitled "The Communication of Suicidal Intent: A Study of 134 Consecutive Cases of Successful (Completed) Suicide" (1959), gives three brief case histories, representative of three diagnostic categories of suicide (manic-depressive depression, chronic alcoholic, and miscellaneous group), to demonstrate the communication of suicidal intent by these persons. Robins' findings indicated that ". . . 98% of these persons were probably clinically ill prior to their suicides." [50] Sixty-nine per cent had communicated suicidal ideas and forty-one per cent specifically stated they intended to commit suicide.

An interesting article in the light of the previous discussion of Durkheim and the aetiological approach is Litman's investigation of 100 cases of equivocal suicides among adults. The article, "Investigations of Equivocal Suicides" (1963) [51] discusses nine case histories. It brings into question an aspect previously discussed, i.e. how reliable are official suicide rates and by what criteria does one attribute any particular death to suicide?

This sampling is by no means intended as a comprehensive listing of psychiatric case histories on suicides and suicide attempters. It is only given as a representative cross section. The list might easily be extended. [52, 53, 54, 55, 56, 57] However, the number of thorough case histories of suicides covering extended periods of time are as scarce as those offering superficial coverage are plentiful.

Detailed Case Histories

The following are some of the more detailed and useful case histories to be found in the literature. Perhaps the most famous psychiatric case history is "The Case of Ellen West." [58] Here we have a detailed account covering the period from her early childhood to the time of her suicide at the age of 32. The patient's diary and the case reports of her therapists are the principle sources of information.

In Cavan, cases XXIX and XXX, "Marian Blake and her Loves," a case history account of a murder-suicide based primarily on her diary, and "A Youth who was Prematurely Tired," the case history of a suicide, are perhaps the best examples of the invaluable source of data diaries offer.[59] In the first of these, the period covered is from Marian's nineteenth birthday in 1912 to her death in 1917. It is about 50,000 words long, and Cavan offers only an abstract of it in *Suicide* (1928). The second diary covers the nineteen-month period in the life of the victim immediately preceding his suicide at age 23. This is also an excellent first hand account and provides the reader with many insights regarding the suicide's problems.

Kobler and Stotland, in their book *The End of Hope* (1964),[60] have very good detailed case histories for five adults; one had attempted and four had succeeded in suicide during a suicide epidemic in a mental hospital. The book is concerned with an analysis of the sequence of events leading up to the suicides.

Finally, James Jan-Tausch, in a study of suicides among New Jersey public school children from 1960–63, compiled a total of forty-one case histories of suicides. Three of these are included in a report entitled *Suicide of Children 1960–63: New Jersey Public School Students.* An interesting finding in this study in the light of my own work was that

> The most significant factor related to suicide among school children was the relationship between the child and the people with whom he socialized. *In every case of suicide, the child was described as having no close friends with whom he might share confidences or from whom he received psychological support.*[61] [Emphasis added]

Two of the more popular assumptions serving as a basis for "interpreting" these and other case histories are summarized below. One can proceed, as Durkheim did, on the assumption that ". . . all suicides of the insane are either devoid of any motive or determined by purely imaginary motives. *Now, many voluntary deaths fall into neither category; the majority have motives, and motives not unfounded in reality.*" [62] (Emphasis added.) On the other hand, a basically psychological position can be taken, the most popular of which is the frustration-aggression model. The assumptions of the psychoanalytic version are well put by Schechter.

> The dynamics of depression have been well described. In general, in adults, these descriptions have stated that, when an individual's hostility cannot be expressed outwardly, it is turned against the introjected objects, which—because they are a part of the self—results in the attempted or actual destruction of the self. Depressions in children have also been described clinically. While the same dynamic of hostility directed against a formerly loved, but now hated, introjected object is hypothesized, these descriptions have also stressed the factor of the extreme dependence of the child on the parent, his love object. Thus, whenever children feel the threat of the loss of a love object, they not only develop feelings of rage toward the frustrating object, but feelings of helplessness and worthlessness as well. This results in, and is equivalent to, a depression. Actually, these states of affective tension occur in a lesser degree rather frequently during childhood. To deal with these affective states, children learn to utilize a number of defense mechanisms, especially those developed in their personal history and those emphasized in their environment. It is when the degree of tension is extremely high and the defense mechanisms break down or become ineffective that suicide or suicidal equivalents may appear.
>
> Inasmuch as the child is still so dependent upon his love objects for gratifications and as the process of identification has not been completed, turning of the hostility against and destroying the introjects within himself is too painful and too frightening. But another important factor is that the child's size and ego status also militate against the use of specific instruments of destruction. Thus, children rarely commit suicide, or even make overt suicidal attempts or threats, but rather express their self-destructive feelings in other ways. These may be called "suicidal equivalents," that is, attenuated attacks on the introjected object which result in depressions, "accidental" injuries, anti-social acts, and the like— all of which have the potentiality for ending in the destruction of the individual. These partial attacks on the self should be treated with the same caution as the more direct, overt self-destructive act in the adult. In the adolescent the impulses can more easily take the form of overt suicidal acts because of the lessened dependence on the love object (accompanied by the heightened emotional stresses of reawakened oedipal conflicts) and also be-

[margin annotation: Children dependent on love objects]

cause he is now a person physically more capable of hurting himself. In addition, in the actions of the suicidal child can be seen not only the hostility against the frustrating parents turned inward, but also the desperate attempts at regaining contact with the lost gratifying love object. In other words, the suicidal act also represents a type of restitutional phenomenon. It is in this psychoanalytic framework—the attack on the introjected object and the attempts to recover it as a love obejct—that we can best understand some of the suicides or suicidal equivalents of children.[63]

Durkheim's position implies that the individual, in opting for suicide, has made a conscious-rational choice on the basis of motives founded in reality. As such, it is not unreasonable to view suicide in this case as an "adaptive" technique. The psychological position holds that the individual is moved to suicide by some unconscious-irrational "psychodynamics" stemming ultimately from a depression which serves to narrow his field of view on alternatives, which in turn causes suicide to appear as the only choice. Here the suicide (to the extent that a choice can be said to be involved at all) is seen to have "chosen" unconsciously and/or irrationally. He would not have committed suicide if he were rational and conscious of the choices, and as such, the act constitutes a "mal-adaptive" technique. Most psychiatrists and clinical psychologists hold to this view or some variation of it. Some sociologists also adhere to this formulation. Henry and Short, Iga [64] and others are a few examples of sociologists who have integrated a frustration-aggression model into their theories.

Using this theoretical perspective, how successful are psychiatrists in anticipating and/or preventing suicide? Since they are little concerned about social-structural factors to be found in these accounts, or—if they are—therapists tend to "interpret" their "real meaning," independent of "apparent" meaning, it is perhaps not surprising to find that "There is no critical data to support the idea that drugs, electro-shock therapy, or psychotherapy are effective in preventing suicide." [65]

Stengel and Cook state:

> Though none would deny its importance, it must be recognized that statistical data, however interesting, cannot compensate for the ignorance of important aspects of the problem [of suicide] which have so far received comparatively little attention, nor is there yet evidence that psychopathological studies have helped to reduce the suicide rate. Psychopathology has so far been more illuminating with regard to suicidal tendencies as a facet of human behavior than in explaining why suicidal acts occur in certain

individuals. The methods of clinical psychiatry have not materially changed since the first studies.[66]

Indeed a recent follow-up study of 618 suicidal patients, designed to see how many of these patients later succeeded in suicide, and how the successful ones related to their psychiatric diagnosis at the time of their attempt, revealed the following:

> The individual cases were evaluated in terms of the symptoms of depression at the time of the original consultation, regardless of the clinical diagnosis. . . . It is apparent that there is an inverse relationship here, with the slightly depressed having a much higher rate [of suicide] than the seriously depressed.[67]

In conclusion it was noted:

> . . . suicidal behavior (attempts, threats and ideas) is one of the strongest indicators of future suicide—more relevant than psychiatric diagnostic groupings.[68]

To the extent that one views suicide and suicide attempts as serious social problems, I feel we ought to reorient ourselves with respect to future studies of suicide. Notwithstanding the optimistic predictions of some suicide prevention centers (see discussion in Chapter 4 for example), the prospects are not good for suicide prevention, given the existing state of our understanding and the commitments of the social and behavioral sciences to the above theoretical models.

I believe, as Mills did, that the acceptance of a biological model as an explanation of suicide presents the researcher with an insoluble dilemma. The contention of Tabachnick and others [69, 70, 71] that suicide is an unconscious-irrational act, notwithstanding all empirical evidence to the contrary, is a difficult position to maintain. Tuckman et al. ". . . were impressed with the possibility that in a number of cases suicide could have resulted from a conscious 'rational' decision reached by weighing the pros and cons of continuing to live, although to a lesser extent unconscious factors may have been operating." [72] This is especially telling in the light of an assumption made by Tuckman et al. and others that the contents of suicide notes ". . . represents the thoughts and affect of the suicide at the time of note writing and death." [73] Parnell and Skottowe found that "From the preventative point of view, the most significant finding is the small number of [suicidal] patients showing disorders of thinking, the change so often regarded by the general public as sine qua non for admission to a general hospital." [74]

The popular assumptions of the frustration-aggression model as outlined earlier (See Shechter's description), and assumed for example by Henry and Short, Jan-Tausch, or Iga, are no less tenuous. Tuckman *et al.*, in analyzing the emotional contents of 165 suicide notes, found that in only *one per cent* of them was there hostility "turned inward." West found that in 148 cases of murder-suicide it was not hostility so much as despair that was encountered. This finding is significant in the light of the striking similarity West found between the case histories of murder-suicides and suicides. Then, too, there were as many suicide attempts among murderers (aggression turned outward) as there were among suicides (aggression turned inward). Finally, if one still chooses to hold that suicide is an act of hostility, what does it help to explain if we speak of the same person turning aggression outward and then inward in a matter of moments, as in the cases of murder-suicide?

The case for the relationship between insanity and suicide, based on an assumption popular since Esquirol that suicide is either *per se* a form of mental disease, or symptomatic of one, is not very convincing either. One half of the cases in West's sample were declared "sane," while Cavan and Wolfgang contended cases of murder-suicides were rarely insane. Stengel and Cook state with regard to insanity and suicide that:

> Differences between findings have been largely due to differences between the samples under investigation and the diagnostic classifications employed by the various authors, and also to the uncertainties inherent in psychiatric diagnosis. The latter obviously becomes much more hazardous if carried out in retrospect and based on insufficient data. *Nevertheless, there is general agreement that only a minority of those who commit suicide were suffering from a major mental disorder, the proportion of these hardly ever exceeding one-third of the total.*[75] [Emphasis added.]

The advantage to viewing suicide as an "impulsive act" is also difficult to appreciate.[76] Robins, Farberow [77] and others have all made capital of the fact that suicides communicate their intentions in advance. Given this and the fact that so many have previously attempted suicide, what does suicide as an "impulsive act" mean? Impulsive is defined by Webster as "a sudden spontaneous inclination or incitement to some usually unpremeditated action." How can suicide be considered spontaneous and unpremeditated when so many suicides communicate their intentions to others in advance? It is true that not all psychiatrists are committed to the idea that suicides result from an impulsive act. For example, Robert E. Litman, Chief Psychiatrist at the Los Angeles Suicide Prevention Center, has this to say:

> Investigations of suicide deaths reveal that, *in the great majority of cases, suicide did not occur suddenly, impulsively, unpre-*

dictably or inevitably, but was, on the contrary, the final step or outcome of a progressive failure of adaptation.[78] [Emphasis added]

Finally, the concept of "depression" as it pertains to suicide also seems very questionable. It is a truism to say that many experience depression who do not attempt suicide. In fact, Pokorny found an inverse relationship between the intensity of depression in suicidal patients and those who later committed suicide.

The "sociological" findings of those following in Durkheim's footsteps are also plagued by serious problems. Quite apart from whether or not their findings tend to support one another (see the discussion earlier in the chapter) Durkheim, Henry and Short, Gibbs and Martin, *et al.* have many an intra-system dilemma. In addition to the logical inconsistencies within their respective "systems" (see pages 6–8), there is the more general problem of validity (see Douglas' Critique page 6) in using official statistical rates of suicide as a source of data.

CONCLUSIONS

Existing sociological and psychiatric explanations of suicide are not very helpful in explaining why one person resorts to suicide and another does not. What is indicated is the need for a new perspective, or, more correctly, the reinstitution of an old and untried one. Since statements imputing motives to "prior," biological, or "deeper" causes are not given to empirical falsification, they must remain what they are (creative or otherwise), metaphysical speculations. There are two sources of data relevant to the problem of suicide which lend themselves to empirical study. These are the chronological ordering of social-structural events found in the detailed accounts of the suicide's biography as he related them, or his conscious verbalizations as related by him either in direct interviews or suicide notes. What I have done is to study adolescent suicide and suicide attempts from the general perspective of the morphological approach while incorporating the above forms of data.

By this approach, I believe I have gained greater insight into the question of why suicidal acts occur with certain individuals and not others than is currently provided by traditional sociological or psychiatric explanations. I feel Durkheim was correct to consider suicide as a social fact whose antecedents would be found in previous social facts. However, it is my contention that he prematurely abandoned the morphological approach and with it the search for a common denominator to suicide. This he would have found in the life histories of suicides, their diaries and suicide notes had he availed himself of this data and held to the form of analysis he avowed early in *Suicide*, i.e. the morphological approach.

FOOTNOTES

1. *Suicide Among Youth,* A Supplement to the Bulletin of Suicidology (Washington, D.C.: U.S. Government Printing Office, 1969), prepared by Richard A. Seiden, pp. 22, 21, 25, respectively.

2. Emile Durkheim, Suicide: *A Study in Sociology* (New York: Free Press, 1951), p. 146.

3. *Ibid.,* pp. 146–147.

4. *Ibid.,* p. 147.

5. *Ibid.,* p. 146.

6. *Ibid.,* p. 62.

7. Jack P. Gibbs and Walter T. Martin, *Status Integration and Suicide* (Eugene: University of Oregon Press, 1964).

8. Andrew F. Henry and James F. Short, *Suicide and Homicide* (Glencoe, Illinois: The Free Press, 1954).

9. Elwin H. Powell, "Occupational Status and Suicide: Toward a Redefinition of Anomie," *American Sociological Review,* XXIII (April, 1950), 131–139.

10. Durkheim, *op. cit.,* pp. 41–42.

11. *Ibid.,* p. 44.

12. *Ibid.,* p. 44. It would seem that this would omit the insane, to the extent that their acts were automatic or impulsive, since they could not have been aware of their consequences in advance. All four forms of suicide that Durkheim used to classify the insane, and which he believed "probably include the most important varieties," fell under this heading. "Maniacal," "melancholy," "obsessive" and "impulsive" forms of suicide all had in common a lack of motive. "In short, all suicides of the insane are either devoid of any motive or determined by purely imaginary motives." It follows from this that suicide among the insane is a contradiction in terms, since they must know the consequences of their act in advance and all four categories of insanity noted above specifically exclude this possibility.

13. Jack D. Douglas, *The Social Meanings of Suicide* (Princeton, New Jersey: Princeton University Press, 1967), p. 203.

14. Henry and Short, *op. cit.,* p. 13.

15. Jacob Tuckman, Robert J. Kleiner and Martha Lavell, "Emotional Content of Suicide Notes," *American Journal of Psychiatry,* July 1959, p. 61.

16. D. J. West, *Murders Followed by Suicide* (London: Heinimann, 1965), p. 142.

17. *Ibid.,* p. 145.

18. *Ibid.,* p. 146.

19. *Ibid.,* p. 143.

20. *Ibid.,* pp. 9, 11. This is of particular interest in light of what is likely to become one of the most famous cases of murder-suicide, that of Charles Whitman at the University of Texas. Typical of murder-suicides, he was before the fact considered a model citizen. After the fact, the grand jury report on the case, cited in *The New York Times* of August 3, 1966, called Whitman a "crazy, deranged" man. Governor Connally of Texas, commenting on the suicide notes Whitman left, said the notes were penned "by a man with a deranged mind." These opinions were followed by Austin's Chief of Police, Bob Miles who said: "Considering that the subject was irrational, he was very rational in his notes. He had just decided that this world was not worth living in."

21. James Jan-Tausch, "Suicide of Children 1960–63, New Jersey Public School Studies" (Bulletin put out by State of New Jersey, Department of Education), p. 10.

22. Jack P. Gibbs and Walter T. Martin, "A Theory of Status Integration and Its Relationship to Suicide," *American Sociological Review,* April 1958, p. 140.

23. *Ibid.,* p. 141.

24. *Ibid.,* p. 142.

25. *Ibid.,* p. 142.

26. Powell, *op. cit.,* pp. 131–139.

27. A. L. Porterfield, "Suicide and Crime in the Social Structure of an Urban Setting: Fort Worth 1930–1950," *American Sociological Review,* XVII (1952), 341–343.

28. Ruth S. Cavan, *Suicide* (Chicago: University of Chicago Press, 1928), p. 105.

29. Powell, *op. cit.,* pp. 131–139.

30. Peter Sainsbury, *Suicide in London* (Chapman and Hall Ltd., 1955), p. 90.

31. Durkheim, *op. cit.,* pp. 297–298.

32. See Jerry Jacobs, "The Use of Religion in Constructing the Moral Justification of Suicide," in *Social Construction of Moral Meanings,* edited by Jack D. Douglas (New York: Basic Books, 1970), for a description of how the study of "moral casuistry" can be used to explain social suicide-rates.

33. Ludwig Binswanger, "The Case of Ellen West," *Existence,* eds. Rollo May *et al.* (New York: Basic Books, 1958), p. 258.

34. Durkheim, *op. cit.,* p. 298.

35. E. S. Shneidman and N. L. Farberow, "Suicide and Death," *The Meaning of Death,* ed. H. Feifel (New York: McGraw-Hill Books Inc., 1959), pp. 287–288.

36. Erwin Stengel, *Suicide and Attempted Suicide* (Baltimore: Penguin Books, 1964), p. 45.

37. Norman Tabachnick, "Observations on Attempted Suicide," *Clues to Suicide* (New York: McGraw-Hill Book Co., Inc., 1957), pp. 167–168.

38. E. Stengel and Nancy Cook, *Attempted Suicide* (London: Chapman and Hall, 1958), p. 14.

39. C. Wright Mills, "Situated Actions and Vocabularies of Motive," *American Sociological Review,* V, No. 6 (December 1940), 909.

40. Merton J. Kahne, "Suicide Research: A Critical Review of Strategies and Potentialities in Mental Hospitals," *The International Journal of Social Psychiatry,* XII, No. 2 (Spring 1966), 120–129.

41. Theodore Lidz, "Adolph Meyer and the Development of American Psychiatry," *The American Journal of Psychiatry,* CXXIII:3 (September 1966), 326.

42. *Ibid.,* p. 331.

43. Stengel *et al., op. cit.,* p. 39.

44. Joseph D. Teicher and Jerry Jacobs, "Adolescents Who Attempt Suicide: Preliminary Findings," *American Journal of Psychiatry,* CXXII:11 (May 1966), 125–6.

45. Stengel *et al., op. cit.,* p. 76.

46. Warren A. Stearns, "Cases of Probable Suicide in Young Persons Without Obvious Motivation," *The Journal of the Maine Medical Association,* XLIV (1953), 16–23.

47. Cavan, *op. cit.,* pp. 198–244.

48. West, *op. cit.*

49. Harold Greenwald, *The Call Girl* (New York: Ballantine Books, 1958).

50. Eli Robins *et al.*, "The Communication of Suicidal Intent: A Study of 134 Consecutive Cases of Successful (Completed) Suicide," *The American Journal of Psychiatry*, CXV, No. 8 (February 1959), 724–733.

51. Robert E. Litman *et al.*, "Investigations of Equivocal Suicides," *The Journal of the American Medical Association*, CLXXXIV (June 22, 1963), 924–929.

52. Albert Schrut, "Suicidal Adolescents and Children," *The Journal of the American Medical Association*, CLXXVIII (June 29, 1964), 1103–1107.

53. Percy Mason, "Suicide in Adolescents," *Psychoanalytic Review*, XLI (1954), 48–54.

54. Henry I. Schneer *et al.*, "Events and Conscious Ideation Leading to Suicidal Behavior in Adolescence," *Psychiatric Quarterly*, XXXV (1961), 507–515.

55. B. C. Bosselman, *Self-Destruction: A Study of the Suicidal Impulse* (Springfield, Illinois: Charles A. Thomas Publisher, 1958).

56. Harold Jacobziner, "Attempted Suicides in Adolescence," *The Journal of the American Medical Association*, CLIXI (January 4, 1965), 7–11.

57. Lauretta Bender and Paul Schilder, "Suicidal Preoccupations and Attempts in Children," *American Journal of Orthopsychiatry*, VII, No. 2 (1939), 225–233.

58. Binswanger, *op. cit.*, pp. 237–267.

59. Cavan, *op. cit.*, pp. 198–244.

60. Arthur L. Kobler and Ezra Stotland, *The End of Hope* (Glencoe, Illinois: The Free Press, 1964).

61. Jan-Tausch, *op. cit.*, p. 3.

62. Durkheim, *op. cit.*, p. 66.

63. Marshall D. Schechter, "The Recognition and Treatment of Suicide in Children," *Clues to Suicide*, eds. Edwin Shneidman and Norman Faberow (New York: McGraw-Hill Book Co., Inc., 1957), p. 131.

64. Mamoru Iga, "Suicides of Japanese Youths," *Sociology and Social Research*, XLVI, No. 1 (October, 1961), 88.

65. A comment by Eli Robins in an article entitled "Potential Suicides—What to look for," *The Journal of the American Medical Association*, CXCIV, No. 9 (November 29, 1965), 27.

66. Stengel *et al.*, *op. cit.*, p. 17.

67. *Alex D. Porkony*, "A Follow Up Study of 618 Suicidal Patients," *The American Journal of Psychiatry*, CXXII (10), (1966), 1114.

68. *Ibid.*, p. 1116.

69. *Tabachnick*, *op. cit.*, pp. 167–168.

70. Charles William Wahl, "Suicide as a Magical Act," *Clues to Suicide*, eds. Edwin Shneidman and Norman Farberow (New York: McGraw-Hill Book Co., Inc., 1957), p. 23.

71. Stengel *et al.*, *op. cit.*, p. 45.

72. Tuckman *et al.*, *op. cit.*, p. 62.

73. *Ibid.*, p. 59.

74. R. W. Parnell and I. Skottowe, "Toward Preventing Suicide," *Lancet*, I (1967), pp. 206–208.

75. Stengel *et al.*, *op. cit.*, p. 14.

76. Bosselman, *op. cit.*, and Jacobziner, *op. cit.*

77. Robins, *op. cit.*, February 1959 and Norman L. Farberow, "The Suicidal Patient and the Physician," *Mind,* I:69 (March 1963), pp. 65–75.

78. A comment by Robert E. Litman in an article entitled "Potential Suicides—What to Look for," *The Journal of the American Medical Association,* CXCIV, No. 9 (November 29, 1965), 27.

CHAPTER 2

Theoretical-Methodological Orientation

The author's general theoretical orientation is based upon a formulation derived by Cressey in his study of embezzlement. Cressey states:

> ... the central problem is to account for the differential in behavior indicated by the fact that some persons in positions of financial trust violate that trust, whereas others in identical or very similar positions do not violate it.[1]

The notion of "trust violation" was of particular interest to the author. Stated in its final form, the hypothesis reads:

> Trusted persons become trust violators when they conceive of themselves as having a financial problem which is non-shareable, are aware that this problem can be resolved by violation of the position of financial trust, and are able to apply to their own conduct in that situation the verbalizations which enable them to adjust their conceptions of themselves as users of the entrusted funds or property.[2]

LIFE AS A SACRED TRUST

On the basis of this formulation, the author was led to ask the following questions. What non-shareable problems do suicides or suicide attempters have? How could these be secretly resolved by an act of trust violation (suicide) where the person violates the sacred trust of life; and what verbalizations do they apply to their intended act that allows them to adjust their conception of themselves as trusted persons with their behavior as trust violators?

Like Cressey, I sought to answer these questions by interviewing fifty persons, adolescent suicide attempters, (and at least one parent) within forty-eight hours of the attempt. However, unlike Cressey's work the author's study incorporates a high order probability model and control group as opposed to the methodological procedures of "Analytic Induction."[3]

26

The main objective of the study was to establish, on the basis of the information given me in the interviews, the formal aspects of the process to which the suicide attempters were subject. To accomplish this, the author would first have to uncover the range of unshareable problems the adolescents experienced and why they were unshareable. Were their problems so horrendous that one would not reasonably be expected to share them, or was it rather that the adolescent felt there was no one available to share them with? In the event of the latter, what sequence of events had the suicide attempters experienced that would lead them to feel socially isolated from meaningful social relationships? Was there anything that the suicide attempters, as a group, had experienced that the control adolescents had not, that would lead them to feel these unshareable problems could be resolved through the violation of a trust—suicide? Given that most people at some time consider suicide, fewer attempt it, and very few accomplish it, what is the process of verbalizations one must entertain in order to be able to act upon one's consideration of suicide?

While the author's work was not based upon an "Analytic Induction" model it did seek to find *a common denominator* to suicide *in a process,* and hoped to uncover this process *in the verbatim accounts of the attempters themselves.* The extent to which the adolescent suicide attempters were found to be subject to a common process would be expressed in terms of a probability statement. In brief, I sought to answer the questions posed on page 26 and hoped to uncover them by comparing the case histories of fifty adolescent suicide attempters with case histories of fifty "normal" adolescents. Individuals were matched on age, race, sex, and level of mother's education.

CENTRAL HYPOTHESIS

Based upon an analysis of the case histories the author derived the following central hypothesis:

Adolescent suicide attempts result from the adolescent feeling that he has been subject to a progressive isolation from meaningful social relationships. The formal aspects of this process are outlined below. The adolescent must have experienced:

1. A long-standing history of problems (from early childhood to the onset of adolescence).
2. The escalation of problems (since the onset of adolescence) above and beyond those usually associated with adolescence.
3. The progressive failure of available adaptive techniques for coping with the old and new increasing problems which leads to the

adolescent's progressive isolation from meaningful social relationships.

4. A chain reaction dissolution of any remaining meaningful social relationships in the days and weeks preceding the attempt which leads to the adolescent's feeling that he has reached "the end of hope."

5. The internal process by which he justifies suicide to himself, and thus manages to bridge the gap between thought and action.

THE SAMPLE

The task of acquiring fifty adolescent suicide attempters and their parents for interview within forty-eight hours of the attempt presented less of a problem than the author at first supposed. The study was conducted at the Los Angeles County General Hospital under the auspices of the Department of Psychiatry of the University of Southern California's School of Medicine.[4] The author was employed at the time as a Research Associate and Co-Director of the project. During the period of September 1964 to May 1965, the author acquired a sample of 50 adolescents who were treated at the hospital's emergency room for suicide attempts. Prior to this, (from January to September 1 of 1964) 48 other adolescent suicide attempters were seen. These 48 cases were not included as a part of the study sample. The insight and data gained from interviewing these adolescents and their parents were useful in helping to decide the final theoretical-methodological perspective of the study, and they also provided an invaluable source of aid in designing and pretesting the instruments to be used on the study sample.

The acquisition of 50 adolescent suicide attempters under these conditions was, however, subject to certain administrative constraints. For example, since all of these cases were placed on a seventy-two hour "voluntary hold" for observation on the adolescent ward of the psychiatric unit, they had to be between the ages of fourteen and eighteen and not "visibly pregnant." Another constraint was that the adolescents becoming part of the sample not be "mentally retarded," in order that they be able to understand and answer the questions put to them by the interviewers. Only one teenager was disqualified on this count. Since participation in the study was on a voluntary basis, some adolescents seen for a suicide attempt chose not to participate. It is interesting to note in this regard that the only ones choosing not to participate were three cases of upper class adolescents.[5] The adolescents who did volunteer, (with their parents' consent) were cooperative. As a rule, the parent (usually the mother) was less free than the adolescent in volunteering information. Fathers were interviewed in only two cases. There was a general reluctance among fathers to participate in the study.

If the suicide attempters were acquired with relative ease, acquiring a control group for the study proved to be a considerable undertaking. Many inquiries were made of various school districts and social organizations. Every agency contacted and informed of the study's purpose considered it a very worthwhile piece of research with many important implications for securing a better understanding of adolescent problems, not the least of which was "dropping out." However, none agreed to participate and all for the same reason. What if one of the adolescents participating in the study should attempt or succeed in suicide? Even if their participation in the study had nothing whatever to do with it, the burden of responsibility and unfavorable publicity would fall upon the shoulders of the agency that had agreed to his participation in the research.

It was nearly a year before the author acquired access to a control group. This occurred as the result of fortuitous circumstances when it was discovered that one of the psychiatrists at the hospital who took an interest in the study was a personal friend of a suburban high school principal. After several meetings with members of the Board of Education, as well as the Principal and Vice-Principal, the author was allowed access to the school population. The Principal agreed to make the student body aware of the study and solicit their support. It was presented as a "Study of Adolescence," and five dollars was offered to those participating for every completed interview with the teenager and his parent. These were conducted simultaneously, but separately, by two trained interviewers in the participant's home. A total of 31 adolescents and their parents were interviewed.

Every effort was made to match the suicide attempters and control group as closely as possible. In this regard the crucial question is, how well were the "matched pairs" matched on the variables chosen to act as indicators of comparable "life chances," i.e., age, race, sex, and level of mother's education. The answer is, very closely. Twenty-six out of the thirty-one cases were matched one to one on race, sex and mother's education. All were also very closely matched by age. In fact, the average difference in age between the experimental and control groups is "0." Both had a mean age of 16. The remaining five cases were equally well matched, with the exception of mother's education. However, since the mothers of two of the suicide attempters and those of three control adolescents had a higher level of education, one would expect any biasing effect on the group data resulting from the differentials in these five cases to be virtually nil. (See Table I in the appendix for a description of the matched pairs.)

In addition to being matched on the above variable, there were the serendipitous findings that the control group also had a high rate of broken homes, both parents working, relatives coming to live with the family, etc. The average difference in net family income between the experimental and control groups was within $100 per month. *Most important is the fact that the number of studies dealing directly with adolescent suicide attempters and their parents immediately following the attempt and using a control group are virtually non-existent; in fact, to the best of the author's knowledge this study was the first.* The hazards of inferring from the case histories of suicide attempters (almost all of those which are found in the literature are reconstructed ex post facto on the basis of official records rather than actual interviews) the "cause" of the attempt, without the benefit of a control group for comparison, will be graphically illustrated in the discussion of the myth of "broken homes" in Chapter 3.

METHODS OF DATA COLLECTION

Each adolescent in the experimental group was interviewed within 24–48 hours of the actual suicide attempt by the sociologist or his research assistant and a psychiatrist. The structured interview schedule used covered the following areas: the suicide attempt, family relations, peer relations, attitudes toward and performance in school, and career aspirations. The attempter's parent was also interviewed using a structured interview schedule which covered the same areas but with an additional section on the adolescent's "developmental" history. Each interview required about one and a half hours to complete.

Both adolescent and parent completed identical sections in the interview schedules covering behavioral problems and disciplinary techniques, which provided essentially two separate versions of these situations. The teenagers in the control group and their parents received the same interviews as the suicide attempters, minus the section on the suicide attempt itself. They also completed the sections on behavioral problems and disciplinary techniques.

Therapy was offered to each adolescent suicide attempter. All of the attempters were seen at least once (following the attempt) by a psychiatrist. Thirty-two of these initial psychiatric interviews were tape recorded and transcribed.

The data received from the sociological interviews was put into case history form according to a standard format based on the five areas mentioned above. An attempt was made to thus place the data in the context of the adolescent's total biography where particular attention could then be directed not only to the events, but, more significantly, to their sequential ordering. These data took the form of two stories: the parents' biography of the adolescent and the adolescent's autobiography. The two comprised a single case history. Additionally, information obtained from an analysis of transcriptions made of taped therapy sessions, suicide notes written by the attempter to parents or boyfriends, and letters or outside information received from others after the fact, were also incorporated into the case histories when available.

On the basis of these case histories, incorporating the above sources of data, a life history chart was constructed for each experimental and control adolescent. This was done by putting all of the events recorded in the case history into chronological order along a vertical continuum depicting graphically the experiences of the adolescent from birth until the time of the last suicide attempt (forty-three per cent had more than one attempt). In addition, whatever background information was obtained from the parent interviewed was also included in the life history chart. A condensed version of the form the charts took is presented below.

They depict graphically and in considerable detail the life histories of both the suicide attempters and control adolescents. The dots appear in different colors and markings representing nineteen categories of events, e.g., residential moves, school changes, onset of various behavioral prob-

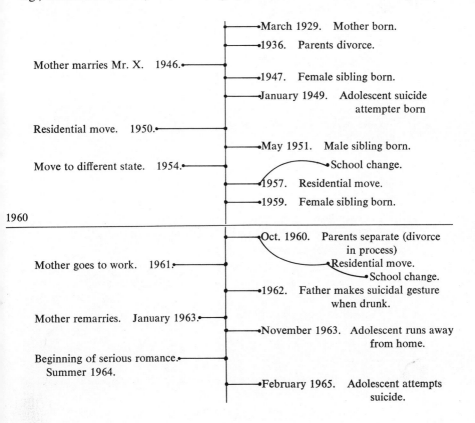

lems, separation or divorce of parents, acquisition of a stepparent, deaths in the family, and suicide attempts.

By comparing the distribution of the colored dots and the comments accompanying them for the suicide attempters and control group, *we can see not only what was experienced by the two sets of adolescents but, more significantly, what the sequential ordering of these events was and how they tended to "pile up" or not, depending on their chronology.* This allows us to view the "precipitating cause" not as a particular isolated crisis, but within the context of the adolescent's total biography. *From this perspective the adolescent no longer seems to be attempting suicide over some trivial isolated problem. The findings also seriously call into question the notion that adolescent suicide attempts are essentially unconscious, irrational, maladaptive or impulsive in nature.*

I feel I should acquaint the reader at this point with a typical case history of an adolescent suicide attempter taken from the author's series. It is primarily upon an analysis of these case histories that my thesis rests and I feel it is important that the reader be familiar with their general form and content. I am hopeful that such a presentation will serve three main purposes:

1. Provide the reader with a model of the format used, and the areas covered in the case histories,
2. Offer a means of comparing these life histories with those of the "superficial" type cited in the previous chapter, and
3. Offer the reader some insight into the problem of primarily lower class adolescents, and the ways in which they attempted to cope with them.

A non-superficial case history, ought, I believe, to fulfill as many of the following conditions as possible:

1. The account ought to be autobiographical and, if possible, corroborated by another in order to insure against distortions in memory, selective perceptions, etc.
2. The account ought to cover the events in the life of the individual from birth on, as opposed to only a particular brief segment or segments of time.
3. The life history should be as complete and detailed as possible, not only in the number of events included in the account, but also with respect to how the individual felt about these events as they happened.
4. Particular attention ought to be paid to the dates of the events in order to be able to reconstruct not only the occurrences and how they were "experienced," but their sequential ordering.

Based on the above criteria, several good sources of data are diaries, letters written over time to people with whom the letter writer felt free to express himself, verbatim accounts taken from therapy sessions, informal interviews the individual volunteered for or was anxious to participate in, and suicide notes.

A CASE HISTORY OF AN ADOLESCENT SUICIDE ATTEMPTER

The following is a case history of a 15-year-old Caucasian girl who, on November 9, 1964, attempted suicide by swallowing a large number of pain pills of an unknown description that she received earlier for the treatment of a backache. Outlining the adolescent's account (and that of her mother) we find that the events leading up to the attempt took this general course:

1. Carla was left alone at home for the weekend while her mother and new boyfriend went off for a trip to Mexico. (From the mother we learned that Carla felt lonely and called a girl friend and asked her to come over. The friend refused.)
2. Carla had a fight that week with her mother that revolved around Carla's desire to return to her Aunt and Uncle's home in Oregon where she had spent six months (about one and a half years ago). Her 12 year-old brother still resides there. (From the mother we learn Carla and the brother were sent to the Aunt's home at that time because the mother had a breakdown resulting from the loss of a child at birth.)
3. Last week Carla had cut classes for two and a half days staying around the house trying to intercept a letter the Aunt was supposed to send which contained travel money for Carla to come to Oregon. (The Aunt finally wrote saying Carla couldn't come.) At that point Carla's mother said, "If you leave home, you can come back for my funeral."
4. As a result of cutting classes, Carla was sure she would be asked to return to her old high school which she hated. This would of course mean leaving behind her new friends. (She had just completed a move, her 13th, and was at the new school on a "temporary permit.")
5. Also during that week her gym teacher and confidant had been killed in an auto accident. (From the mother we learn that Carla was "unusually easy-going" that week even though she was being punished for forging a letter of excuse to the school principal and signing her mother's name to it. The punishment consisted of being put on "total restriction," i.e., no phone calls, dates, seeing friends or going anywhere for a week's time.)

6. Her mother had married twice before and was preparing to marry soon for a third time to her current boy friend.

7. Carla's real father left home 13 years ago when she was 2 years old.

8. Carla hates her mother and stepfather.

9. Her mother stated that Carla was aware that she (Carla's mother) had previously attempted suicide and that the stepfather's mother and grandmother were both suicides. Carla sometimes chided her mother on her attempt.

10. Carla used to belong to many clubs, had close friends, and was very happy while with her aunt in Oregon. Since her return to Los Angeles (and to her mother) a year and a half ago she has been unhappy, has only one close friend (whom she didn't confide in) and belongs to no school or outside social groups or organizations.

11. She used to be an A student when in grammar school. Now Carla gets just "average grades." Her school attendance (according to the mother) has also suffered recently.

12. All of her "behavioral problems" and the resulting "disciplinary techniques" used by the parent to counter them, and all that cycle implies (see pages 68–73) also began upon her return from Oregon, i.e., within the last one and a half years.

13. Monday morning Carla woke up, and having decided the night before to kill herself, went to school, and took a bottle of assorted pills in an attempt to take her life. (From the mother we learn that before going to school she called her boy friend and told him of her plans to take the pills. He didn't believe her and did nothing about it.)

All in all, one is struck by the number and ordering of the unwanted and unanticipated events experienced by the adolescent and how they led her to experience a progressive isolation from meaningful social relationships. It was this that led her in desperation to attempt suicide. Further, the difference in perception between the mother and daughter, with respect to the daughter's situation, was as striking as the negative consequences resulting from it.

Interview with Carla Brown

The Suicide Attempt

The attempt took place on Monday, November 9, 1964, at 8:30 a.m. at a drinking fountain in the hallway of Suberbia High School. The suicide attempter gave the following account of the twenty-four hours preceding the attempt. On Saturday her mother and the mother's new boyfriend told Carla they wanted to go to San Diego and Tijuana for the weekend. The mother was reluctant to leave Carla alone but she assured her mother it was fine. (She would be spared having to hear her mother's arguments for a day.) The mother left on her trip Saturday afternoon about 1:00 p.m. Carla spent Saturday at home listening to the radio and reading magazines. On Sunday she "didn't feel well" so she stayed home again listening to the radio and reading magazines all day. Mother came back Sunday afternoon. She didn't discuss the trip with her mother at all. Later, she went to the store to get her mother some envelopes; stopped at girlfriend's house to watch the Beatles on T.V. for ten or fifteen minutes, and then returned home and went to bed. That night, "twelve hours" before taking the pills, at about 8:30 p.m., Sunday evening, Carla decided to go to school the following day, take the pills and kill herself. She woke up Monday morning, met her girlfriends as usual, went for a ride around the school as they usually did and started to go to class. That day, before going to class, the suicide attempter had to go to the attendance administrator to get a pass. [She had cut school for two days last week and needed a pass to get in. Since she had only cut school two and a half days in her life, these two days were important.] The week of the attempt Carla had a fight with her mother. She wanted to return to Oregon to her aunt and uncle and 12 year-old brother. She had spent six months there and was very happy. She had been very unhappy since her return to L.A. about one and a half years ago. The mother told her if she left home, she need never return (except for the mother's funeral). Carla called her aunt in Oregon who said she would send her travel money so that she could get there. She stayed home those two days in order to intercept the mailman and get the letter before her mother did.

At school Carla left her friends for a moment, went to the drinking fountain, took the pills, and then cheerfully said, "O.K., let's go to the Attendance Office." Carla knew on Friday that because of cutting classes she would be asked to leave Suberbia High where she was attending on a "district permit," and return to another high school which she had been to previously and hated. Carla had *one* very good friend who was a member of the group of girls waiting for her. Knowing this girl would tell on her to save her life, she told another not so good friend (who she knew wouldn't tell on her), that she took the pills. The girl never did tell. Carla expected when she saw the attendance officer that she would not get a pass to class, but would be told to return to the other school. While talking to the attendant she excused herself to go to her locker. The attendant followed her, saw a lot of empty pill bottles, and told her to come back in the office; she refused and walked away. The attendant following in his car picked her up two blocks from school, surmised she took pills and brought her to Green Hills Hospital where her stomach was pumped.

Carla would not say why she wanted to kill herself. She did say it was not the fight with her mother, the desire to return to Oregon, or the move back to the high school she hated that was the cause. At this point she cried and would not reveal the real reason she took the pills.

She knew 12 hours before the attempt that she would take the pills and all indications are she intended to kill herself. No one saw her take the pills and she told one other girl who told no one else. She had never made a previous attempt. When asked if she would attempt it again she said, "Well, I'll never use pills again," because of the unpleasant experience of having her stomach pumped and because they didn't work. She then added (not too convincingly) that since she was too chicken to cut her wrists, she probably would never attempt it again. (The implication that pills and wrist cutting are the only way for teenage girls to attempt suicide is interesting.)

Carla said her first thoughts about death came one and a half years ago when she was being seen off at the bus station in Oregon by her friends, on returning to L. A. against her will. One of the friends said to call when she got to L. A. She said she would write a card on the bus because she would never live long enough to get to L. A. because the bus would crash. She is convinced she will die in an auto crash. She tells her friends this when they sit around and discuss the way in which each of them will die. This discussion is sometimes triggered while listening to a record by Jimmy Wilson, "The Last Kiss." (Many teenage popular songs deal with death.) Her friend wants to die holding her pet stuffed animal because she is afraid of the dark. She envisioned death while being attacked by a great monster, so that at least the last moment of life would be exciting.

When asked if anyone in the family had attempted suicide or made threats, etc., she gave the following account: Her grandfather had slit her grandmother's throat, her great grandmother had been the victim of an ax murder, three of her aunts committed suicide, one when her husband drowned, and her mother had attempted suicide five years ago when she was in the fifth grade. At this time she came home and found a suicide note telling the stepfather to send the stepson and Carla to the aunt in Oregon. The mother survived. Carla doesn't know why or how her mother attempted suicide. The above account was corroborated by her mother. Carla used the pills she obtained while spending a week in the hospital for a hurt back and kidney infection, October 6 to 13. She would not discuss this. She stated she went to the mountains with her boyfriend and her cousin and her boyfriend recently. It is not clear if this is the same boyfriend she had in April of 1964 who was older (21 years old) and whom she doesn't see anymore.

School, Career, Peer

Carla stated the following with regard to school: She is presently in Suberbia High and about to be transferred for having cut two days, as well as the time she lost during the recent suicide attempt. She is in the 10th grade. Her last semester's grades were under par for her (A, B, C, D, B, F) because she didn't expend much effort, "I didn't care." In grammar school she was an A student without trying but in high school one has to try to continue to be an A student and she doesn't care enough to try. She expects to graduate from high school, and get a couple of years of junior college in order to become either a lab technician or legal secretary. She is presently taking typing and biology in high school with this in mind. Carla generally enjoys school and so do her friends, primarily because it's a place to see and meet everyone. She likes science best and history least. She enjoyed school most in Oregon, less at Suberbia High, and least of all at the school she is about to be transferred to. This is where she went first on returning to L. A. one and a half years ago, after spending six months in Oregon with her aunt and uncle. She does not participate in school activities or clubs now but did participate in school activities in Oregon. She claims to get along with her classmates, friends and most of her teachers. She confided her troubles to the gym teacher as did many of the other girls. The gym teacher was killed in an auto wreck last week, when (1) she had the big fight with her mother, (2) she cut school two days, (3) she was transferred from Suberbia High, and (4) the big unknown, other reason she "really" took the pills.

Her mother is usually after her to do better in school even when she does pretty well. Most of her friends have been to the Dean's office for talking back to teachers but that is considered routine. Only one friend is in serious trouble and on "school contract." This is also the one who is in trouble with the police and the only *one* with a car. Carla says she knows hundreds of people—almost everyone in Suberbia High. She has only *one* good friend to confide in. (Ironically, when she took the pills she did not confide in this one because she knew she would tell on her.)

As to present jobs or future careers, Carla has never had a full or part-time job except for occasional babysitting. She thinks teenagers never really have to work for any of life's necessities, only for luxuries such as a car. She doesn't know if she could find a job; the situation is very remote to her. She doesn't feel her family's economic situation would hinder her from becoming a lab technician or legal secretary. Race has something to do with it because "Negroes don't stand as good a chance." In terms of ambition Carla would *"never be satisfied"*; she would always want to be better. She feels if she succeeds in becoming what she wants to it will not be as good as her mother did, as an escrow officer, and she quit school when she was sixteen. Mother earns about $300 per month.

Carla stated that the worst things she could do to her friends would be to betray a confidence. She likes her present set of friends, and has had the same ones for one and a half years now. None of them have been in trouble with the law (except the one with the car). Carla used to belong to the Girl Scouts, Youth for Christ, and the Girls Athletic Association, all while in Oregon. Now she belongs to no organization at all. She says she is not religious and feels like a hypocrite when she goes to church because she really doesn't understand or believe. Carla stated she started smoking in April of 1964 when she went with 21 year-old boyfriend. She doesn't see him anymore but kept smoking at a rate of about three packs a week. She doesn't drink or like to, and the only drugs beside aspirin she took were the pills they gave her at the hospital with which she made her suicide attempt.

An average day with friends at school consists of meeting the friend with the car, cruising around the school a while, going to class, passing notes up and back, having a good time in gym, meeting after school at her best friend's (Judy's) house where five or six of them play records, talk about who said what at school; plan for the weekend and discuss the guys they're going with. On vacations or weekends twenty or so boys and girls will go in a group to the football game, and afterwards to the school hangout, a pizza parlor. Sometimes they go to the mountains as she did recently with her boyfriend, the cousin, and her boyfriend.

The Family

Carla's real father left the home about thirteen years ago. She used to see him about once every four or five years. She saw him the last time a few months ago. Mrs. Brown remarried Carla's present stepfather about twelve years ago. Carla hates her stepfather and has always hated him. The mother is getting a divorce soon from this man in order to marry her new boyfriend, whom Carla likes pretty well. But Carla feels she will never benefit from it, since she will be going to college by the time they're married and so it will not affect her one way or the other.

The family picture is grim. Carla's mother and the stepfather were always arguing. He never believed Carla when she told him things and often hit her. The stepfather also used to withhold privileges, yell, nag, and criticize her. The mother would primarily use the discipline of "restriction" i.e. withholding all social privileges, a kind of social excommunication for Carla. The stepfather and mother would often disagree about disciplinary procedures and fight about it. The mother would try to stop the stepfather from hitting her, and would usually succeed by having the stepfather turn his anger on the mother and hit her instead. Carla perceives the stepfather, who is now out of the home, as "nuts" and "weird."

Recently the stepfather paid an unexpected call, found the new boyfriend's clothing around the house, took a knife and shredded all his clothing including the shoes. Had the man been there he might well have been shredded as well.

Carla feels "total restriction" is an unfair discipline. What makes it worse is that she never gets to tell her side of the story. The mother is very strict and holds her to the letter of every agreement they make. Carla listed her "behavior problems" as follows: Disobedience, truancy, running away from home (went to girlfriend's house last month), temper tantrums, lying, cruelty (teasing stepbrother), destructiveness, sassiness, defiance, rebelliousness, and being withdrawn. She claims to have exhibited none of these behaviors before returning from the six months spent in Oregon, where she liked it so well.

The thing she could do to make the stepfather angriest was lie (the very thing he induced her to do since he never believed the truth and always hit her in either case). Disobedience made the mother angriest.

When asked what she could do to make them most *unhappy,* she stammered and couldn't answer.

In terms of affect, Carla said she only showed *anger,* this by yelling back or going to her room. To show love to mother she did nothing. She despises her stepfather. To show disappointment or sadness she went to her room, turned out the lights and listened to the radio by herself. Satisfaction and happiness she showed, or one was to surmise, when she was in a good mood. Carla really didn't know how the stepfather felt about the mother because he "acts weird." She knew he didn't care about her because he told her so; but she thinks he "cares" for his son. The mother argues with the stepfather all the time and Carla thinks her mother probably "cares for her and stepbrother." As a special problem Carla states stepfather wants her to visit him or talk to him on the phone. But when she does either he only yells and rants at her. She never wants to see him again.

Conclusion

Carla has had a chaotic home life, full of strife, nagging and lack of trust. In the last month she cut school two days (a unique occurrence), had a big fight with her mother about returning to Oregon, her gym teacher and confidant was killed in car accident, and she was transferred out of school. Between herself and her stepfather there was no communication. The mother is viewed as "caring" but strict and arbitrary. The stepfather is untrusting and "weird," the mother strict and unreasonable. Carla has only one good friend, and that one she didn't confide in prior to the suicide attempt. The "real reason" she attempted suicide remains untold. There certainly seems sufficient reason as is but "the reason" remains a secret Carla is reluctant to part with.

Interview with Mrs. Brown, Mother of Carla Brown

Mrs. Brown is a 32 year-old mother of three who is in the process of divorcing her husband of eleven years, Sam Brown. He is her second husband; a Mr. Jones is the father of Carla and her brother, age 13. Mr. Jones was divorced from Mrs. Brown in 1950. Her third child, a product of the second marriage, is a boy, age 9. Mrs. Brown has a current boyfriend and intends to marry for the third time sometime after this divorce is final.

Daughter's Suicide Attempt

Carla attempted suicide on Monday morning, November 9, 8:30 a.m. in the hallways of Suberbia High School. She swallowed an overdose of pills which had been given her for pain associated with a kidney infection. The day before the suicide attempt Carla was by herself most of the time. Her mother had gone to visit an uncle and Carla didn't want to go. Carla did some household chores (so her mother wouldn't be angry with her, the mother thinks) but laid around in bed most of the day. She has had continuing complaints in connection with a kidney infection—backache, etc. Mrs. B was told by the mother of one of Carla's friends that Carla had called this particular girlfriend and asked her to come over. The girl couldn't come. During the phone conversation Carla made reference to dying— some offhand comment. The friend thought Carla sounded lonesome. (Mother says if she was lonesome she would have come visiting with her.)

Monday morning Carla seemed fine. Her mother dropped her off at school, and was told later that Carla had called her boyfriend at 7:00 a.m. Monday morning and told him that she planned to take the pills. The boy didn't take her seriously, and therefore told no one of her message.

Carla reported to the Vice-Principal's office re discipline over having played hookey. She left the outer office and went into the hall to the water fountain. The Vice-Principal followed, found her at the drinking fountain. She staggered, appeared irrational, and then told him, "I don't have to go back to City High. I took a bottle of pills." The Vice-Principal then called police who in turn took Carla to Green Hills Hospital for stomach pumping. Mother was phoned at work and went to the hospital. The mother accompanied Carla in the ambulance to Los Angeles County General Hospital. Mr. Brown was not informed of the suicide attempt until later.

Carla's mother reports that there were changes in Carla's behavior for several months leading up to the suicide attempt, and that she was aware of some of these changes only because others told her. Carla's aunt told Mrs. B. that "Carla had weird ideas about death." A week before the suicide attempt Carla had been unusually easy-going even though she was being punished. She was not allowed phone calls, dates, etc., for playing hookey and writing (forging) notes from her mother to excuse absences. Carla seemed to accept this restriction complacently. Her mother believes that Carla likes a more strict life than she has had for the last few months. Mr. B. has always been quite strict in the past. (Mr. and Mrs. Brown have not been living together since June.)

One thing that has upset Carla of late is a desire on her part to go to her aunt's place in Oregon and stay with them. Her 13 year-old brother has lived with them since infancy. (When this boy was born, the mother had a nervous breakdown. Her husband had another woman pregnant at the time and was planning to continue his relationship with the other woman, while still supporting Mrs. B. and the babies. The aunt took Carla and the baby boy while the mother recuperated from the breakdown. Carla came back to her mother. The aunt wanted to keep the infant, and the mother allowed it. He thinks of the aunt and uncle as parents.) Carla had stayed with her aunt for one semester until Christmas, 1963. When she first returned to her mother she seemed happy. Then, later, she decided she wanted to go back to Oregon and aunt. Her aunt sent her the money, without the mother's consent, but later called and asked Carla not to come. They had had some financial upset; their money was tied up in investments, and they couldn't afford to take on the added expense of Carla at this time. Carla was very disappointed at this turn of events.

Another unusual behavior was that Carla had been going to her mother's friend's house each afternoon from 4:00 to 5:30 when the mother returned from work. For the few days before the suicide attempt, Carla had not shown up there, but had called her mother at work and asked her to pick her up at a girlfriend's house where she would stay instead. Carla's friends have thought she was disturbed for months. Carla says she hates her mother, doesn't want to live with her. The mother thought perhaps Carla didn't like her new boyfriend, but now it appears she does like him. Carla claims to hate her stepfather, and on two occasions, she approved separations from the stepfather for a year at a time.

When mother asks Carla why she attempted suicide, Carla refuses to talk about it, saying "it's over now, so forget it." Her mother thinks she did it because: "Changing schools upset her, but not entirely. I blame myself for not giving her as much time as I should, but she doesn't want my company. Carla and her brother (9 years old) fight constantly. She's very touchy with him, resents having to care for him. Carla is clever at manipulating social situations so things turn out well for her." (Thus, mother doesn't know why Carla tried to take her life.) Her mother also said she didn't think Carla did intend to die. "She did it to prove a point, that no one can make her do something she doesn't want to do." The mother doesn't think Carla will attempt suicide again; but circumstances which might bring another suicide attempt about are: big enough disappointments. "She can't take disappointment, just like she can't take discipline." (Here we see some strange contradictions. Earlier Mrs. B. said that Carla needed discipline, more strict; now she is saying that Carla can't take discipline.)

Long-term factors re Carla's suicide attempt: her mother had been warned not to get pregnant again after her 9 year-old son was born, because of an Rh factor problem. But she did get pregnant and had a baby boy who lived only 24 hours; this was in January, 1960. Carla was 11 years old at this time and was quite hysterical when the baby died. The mother had "infantile reaction-depression" to this tragedy. She wouldn't leave the house for three months, and finally in March attempted suicide by taking an overdose of pills. Carla knows about this suicide attempt and throws it up to the mother on occasion. When Carla was referred to Los Angeles County General Hospital she wanted to know why so much fuss was being made over her suicide attempt when not much had happened to her mother as a result of her own suicide attempt.

In addition, the stepfather's mother and grandmother each did successfully commit suicide, events of which Carla is aware. The mother admits thinking about suicide attempts in her adolescence, but believes the only time suicide might be a reasonable course of action is for medical reasons, i.e. dying of an incurable disease, or being in great pain. She admits thinking about death often of late. She has a lung problem and feels that she may die anytime. She thinks that she'll miss seeing her grandkids, and that no one would be here to care for Carla. There are no grandparents left really: Mother's own mother is an alcoholic. Carla's mother also admits thinking about suicide in regard to marital problems with second husband.

Behavior Problems and Discipline

The mother describes Carla as engaging in many forms of behavioral problems. Most of Carla's misbehavior, her mother says, occurred in the absence of the stepfather who is a very strict disciplinarian and of whom Carla has always been afraid. Carla was truant two or three times, ran away from home about two months ago, has temper tantrums, lies often, talks back, is generally rebellious and defiant. Mother greatly disapproves of Carla's smoking habit, which she took up because of her friends who are usually older than she is. Carla has "slugged" her mother, and sat on her to prevent mother from hitting her back. "Sassiness" makes her mother most angry; "getting involved with a rough bunch of kids" makes her most unhappy.

Almost every conceivable form of discipline has been tried with Carla. In the last few months her mother has tried to become friends with her. She takes Carla and her friends places. She had no luck at first, but when the friends accepted her mother, Carla was swayed. Carla was formerly critical of her mother and her new boyfriend who she said acted like teenagers, i.e. went dancing, etc. But when Carla's friends voiced approval, Carla thought these things were all right.

Mrs. B. withholds privileges for most serious problems. In the past five months, Carla hasn't been disciplined very often. Her mother tried to understand that Carla was having problems with school. (Carla seemed to disapprove of her mother and her boyfriend. They would hold hands while walking down the street. Mother thinks Carla may be jealous, but Carla doesn't want mother to be alone, either.)

Mr. and Mrs. Brown disagreed almost constantly about disciplining Carla. He picked at her, and nags all the time.

Carla's younger brother, age 9, is a very flighty and emotional child. He flys off the handle, much like the stepfather. He doesn't get along well with other children or with baby-sitters.

Carla's Schooling and Aspirations

Carla is currently enrolled at Suberbia High School, but a transfer back to City High is pending upon her return to school. She had been attending Suberbia on a special permit, because it is out of her residential district now. Carla has attended City for a while, but was very unhappy there. She seemed to have few friends. The transfer back to Suberbia was made, but in the event of any problem, Carla knew she would have to face going back to City. Mother feels Carla is unrealistic regarding her approaching return to Suberbia. She feels Carla will be sent back to City High and will be very upset because of this. But even at Suberbia, Carla feels she is disliked by many of her classmates. She does not belong to the social groups she would like to. She feels rejected.

Over the years, Carla's grades have gotten progressively worse. She was a "straight A" student in grammar school. Now she doesn't do her work and is getting only average grades. Tests in school show she is an intelligent girl, but she won't work. Mrs. B. says she has had trouble getting Carla to attend school this semester.

Carla is very vague about her choice of a future career. Mrs. B. would like her to do some specialized work, whatever Carla would want to do.

Developmental

Although Carla was not a planned pregnancy, Mrs. B. says she looked forward to having the baby and wanted a girl. Mrs. B.'s Rh factor was not a problem at this time. The baby was full term and there was a normal delivery. Just before Carla's birth, Mr. Jones beat Mrs. B., giving her a black eye. When Carla was just three months old, the mother was beaten badly again. Just after Carla's first birthday, Mr. Jones began to spank her with a piece of linoleum. A neighbor and mother stopped him before he hurt her too badly.

Carla was a bottle-baby, a poor eater, but a very active infant. She was weaned at age 2, and stopped wetting the bed at three. Carla has somewhat of a lisp (as does the mother). She has had temper tantrums since age 6 or 7. Carla frequently talks in her sleep (this started about age 6 or 7 and still happens now). She only walked in her sleep once. (The onset of her talking in her sleep seems to correlate with the time when her youngest brother was born.) As a younger child Carla was afraid of someone under her bed. She used to stand several feet from the edge of her bed and leap into it, to avoid getting near the edge.

At age 2 Carla was left with a baby-sitter. When the mother took her home that day she noticed some blood on her training pants. Mother took child to doctor where it was diagnosed that some object had penetrated her hymen, probably a finger. Mother reports that "brother of baby sitter" was taken to jail, but she doesn't know what finally happened to him, because the family moved in the interim. Also, at age 6–7, Carla and some other neighbor's children were observed in sex play. Mothers joined efforts to stop this, but Mrs. B. says Carla was not punished for these things.

At age 11 Carla was instructed re menstruation and reproduction. Mother used library book to help her explain reproduction from lower animals up. This was when mother was pregnant with baby that died. Carla seemed embarrassed by mother's effort to instruct her in sex. Carla began to menstruate at age 13, and did not inform mother until six months later. Mother found this very unusual.

The Family

Since Carla was three and a half years old, Sam Brown has been her stepfather. She has seen her own father off and on several times, but has never lived with him. The nuclear family now consists of: Mrs. Brown, Carla, and Danny (9 years old). Mother plans to remarry soon after the divorce from Mr. Brown is final. The family life has been a series of residential moves, marital shuffling, and generally insecure surroundings. During Carla's lifetime she has moved to about twelve or thirteen houses. Carla's brother (in Oregon) has never lived with the mother and stepfather.

Carla's mother feels that she and Carla have closest relationship in family; and that Mr. B. and Carla have the most problems with each other. Both Mr. and Mrs. B. appear to be immature, childish, unstable people. Mr. B. treats Mrs. B. like a child, and punishes her as such. He seems to fill the "fatherly" role better for Mrs. B. than he does for the "real" children. Carla says she hates her mother, but mother believes Carla loves her; Carla resents her stepfather, thinks he loves Danny but doesn't love her; Carla also resents her stepbrother, thinks mother blames her for Danny's actions. Mother says she loves Carla very much but Carla rejects her. "She'd be better off in Oregon." Not only is Mr. B. involved in treating Mrs. B. as a child, but so is Carla. Carla sometimes hides Mrs. B.'s cigarettes and matches, so she can't smoke. (Mrs. B. has a lung problem which smoking makes worse.) Mrs. B. says Carla wishes her mother was "of a different nature," "more motherly, I guess."

Mrs. B. comes from a broken home herself, and was married for the first time at age 16. She finished the 10th grade in high school and is currently employed as an escrow officer at a Savings and Loan Company. She has worked at six different jobs during Carla's lifetime. Her current income (including child support from Mr. Jones) is about $300 per month. Mr. B. also finished the 10th grade, is currently unemployed. He worked as an operating engineer and was laid off because his company went out of business in October. He has held about six jobs since he's been married to Mrs. B. When he's working he earns "good money, between $500 and $600 a month."

The case history of Carla Brown is typical of the case histories of other adolescent suicide attempters in the author's series with respect to format, length and the extent of descriptive detail.

EXCERPTS FROM THE VERBATIM ACCOUNT
OF A PSYCHIATRIC INTERVIEW

Most of the information contained in the case histories was taken from the structured sociological interviews conducted by the author or his research assistant. As previously noted, the case histories also incorporated data from the transcribed psychiatric interviews, when these provided additional information relating to the sequential ordering of social-structural events in the suicide attempters' lives. An example of a transcribed interview is the following exchange between a 15 year-old suicide attempter and one of the study's psychiatrists.

An analysis of the suicide attempter's account of her circumstances reveals that she had experienced the following set of events which resulted in her progressive isolation from meaningful relationships. The formal aspects of the sequential ordering of these events and their resultant outcomes are the same as those noted in the case history above.

1. Catherine's most recent suicide attempt was her third one.
2. This last attempt was made because her boy friend left her.
3. The second attempt followed her getting drunk and having sexual intercourse with her boy friend (the same boy she refers to now) about three months prior to the last attempt.
4. This, her first encounter with sex, resulted in her becoming pregnant.
5. The pregnancy, in turn, resulted in the breakup of her romance since the boy friend's mother wouldn't let him marry. To make matters worse, Catherine suspects that he may no longer love her because she attempted suicide.
6. The pregnancy also resulted in her further alienation from her mother and stepfather who she already hated and had little contact with. (Her real father left when she was a baby.) For example, Catherine interpreted her mother's concern that she marry the boy friend as an effort on the mother's part to get rid of her.
7. Her mother has been married four times since her real father left, seven times in all.
8. Her sister, to whom she might have been able to confide her problems, takes drugs. Because her boy friend was afraid that Catherine would follow in the sister's footsteps, he asked that she not associate with her too often. Catherine complied.
9. She stopped going to school because a) her peers might learn of the pregnancy, b) she was preoccupied with all of her problems, and c) she lost interest. She used to be a B student but at the time of the attempt was failing. Her lack of attendance resulted in her being isolated even from her casual friends at school.
10. All of her friends were casual friends because losing close friends hurt too much. She knew. She had lost the love of her mother, father and boy friend. She was now in danger of losing her baby as well.
11. She was a very independent girl and didn't ask much from her mother. She would not have received much if she had asked. With Catherine's emancipation the mother asked little of her, i.e., Catherine would not allow herself to be exploited.

12. Even the friendship of pets was denied her. She loved her dog and horse. Her mother was responsible for getting rid of both of them, in spite of Catherine's efforts to keep them.
13. Finally, Catherine reluctantly implies that she will attempt suicide again unless her life's circumstances improve.

In short, the adolescent, through the series of events outlined above (and presented in greater detail in the accounts themselves) experienced a progressive isolation from meaningful social relationships which followed closely the formal aspects of the process described earlier on pages 27–28. It was the sum total of these experiences occurring in the sequence they did that resulted in her suicide attempt.

DR: Catherine, I want to try to understand what it was that brought you to the hospital—what the circumstances were.

TA: I don't know.

DR: You have no idea what it was?

TA: Oh, I don't know. I took some pills—tried to kill myself. And they brought me here.

DR: Could you tell me what kind of pills you took?

TA: I don't know. Some pills the doctor gave me for my stomach for pain, and some aspirins, and sumpin else—some cold tablets, or sumpin, I don't know.

DR: You must have been pretty upset to want to take pills to take your life.

TA: I was.

DR: What were you upset about?

TA: I don't know . . . (pause)

DR: You mean you don't remember what it was?

TA: Yes—I—maybe it was because my boy friend broke up with me.

DR: Had that happened just before this?

TA: It happened that same night.

DR: How did it come about?

TA: I don't know. He got mad cause I went with my sister somewhere—my sister, she stole a car, and she told me to come with her. So we went to mess around in the streets, and so he got mad at me, when he found out about it—and he got mad at me last—Wednesday night, I guess, I can't remember how long I've been here now.

DR: Did it happen last Wednesday night?

TA: I came in Thursday morning, about two o'clock.

DR: So when did you take the pills? Wednesday night? What—did you suddenly decide to take the pills, or had you been thinking about taking them?

TA: No. I just wanted to die right then.

DR: You mentioned your sister had stolen a car. Did you know she had stolen it? Or did you just know it afterwards?

TA: I don't know—I knew—she—she said it was someone else's, but I didn't think—

DR: You rather suspected that she had stolen it?

TA: Well, maybe she stole it off a friend but she didn't particularly want to admit that she took it.

DR: Why was your boy friend so angry?—because it was a stolen car?

TA: He never did like her—she hangs around with some girl—You ain't gonna tell no one what I tell you, are you?

DR: It's just between you and me.

TA: Well, she goes around with this girl that pops her skin and Earl keeps tellin me, don't hang around with her, don't hang around with her—

DR: Popping the skin—you mean taking heroin?

TA: Yes. And he says, don't mess with your sister. She'll get you to do the same thing. Joan hasn't done it—she just smokes the weed now—grass—. And so anyway, I went with her and he thought maybe I did it and he was real mad at me.

DR: Have you ever used the weed?

TA: No! I never would.

DR: Why are you so sure you wouldn't?

TA: Cause—I don't need it.

DR: Do you think your sister NEEDS it?

TA: No, she just—my mom don't care, and Joan's just got in with people and—

DR: Your mom doesn't care? How do you know she doesn't? She doesn't care about you and about your sister?

TA: That's right.

DR: How many sisters and brothers do you have?

TA: Six.

DR: Six?

TA: Four brothers and two sisters.

DR: And how old are they? (TA sighs.) —Starting with the oldest—

TA: Dan I guess is about—well, Mary Ann's 22, and Frank will be 24, and Dan's, he's 26 or 25 or something, and John's 20, and Joan's 17, and I'm 15, and Ben's 3.

DR: I see. I understand, according to your record here, that you've made suicide attempts before, or you've had thoughts about it.

TA: Yes.

DR: How many times have you done this—you're kind of smiling about it—Although, I wonder—I don't think you think it's funny—

TA: I don't care.

DR: Hm?—Maybe you're more embarrassed about it.

TA: I'm not embarrassed—I don't know—it seems kind of funny now.

DR: You mean that you tried to take your life?

TA: Yes.

DR: What were the reasons that you tried to take your life before? . . . Was it again over your boy friend?

TA: Yeah (laughs).

DR: Always over your boy friend? Or were there other people involved?

TA: No. Just him.

DR: Just him, all the time? When was the first time you made a suicide attempt?

TA: I don't know—along about last August—the end of last August.

DR: You mean of this year?

TA: Yeah, this year.

DR: And how did that come about?

TA: I don't know—he—he———oh, one night, we got all drunk and everything, and I had something to do with him, you know, and then, I don't know, next day I was really sorry about it, and I tried to kill myself.

DR: Was that the first time you had something to do with him?

TA: The first and only time. With anybody.

DR: That was pretty upsetting, wasn't it. . . . What happened after that? Do you prefer being called Kate or Kathy?

TA: Call me Mary.

DR: Mary?

TA: Yes.

DR: O.K.

TA: I HATE Catherine.

DR: Mary, how many times did it happen after that?

TA: Once.

DR: Once after that. So it's been three times then?

TA: No—

DR: Counting the other night.

TA: Yeah—

DR: Oh! You mean you had intercourse with him just once after that? Only twice?

TA: Yeah.

DR: You must have gotten pregnant, what, the first time? . . . How do you feel about that?

TA: I don't know . . . I don't feel good.

DR: Were you pretty unhappy about being pregnant? . . . Did you try to do something about the pregnancy?

TA: No. If you're going to have it, you're going to have it. You can't do nothing about it.

DR: But you'd rather you didn't have it? . . . Do you have any plans of what you want to do with the baby?

TA: I dunno.

DR: How far along are you now?

TA: About two months.

DR: About two months. I understand you had some bleeding the other day—

TA: Last Friday.

DR: Are you still bleeding now?—How much?

TA: Not very much.

DR: Enough to wear a pad?

TA: Yeah.

DR: Well, you know what that means, do you?

TA: Yeah.

DR: What does it mean?

TA: It's the start of sort of a miscarriage.

DR: That it's possible, and that's pretty upsetting, too, isn't it?

TA: I wish I'd die with it.

DR: I guess it's upsetting because on the one hand I suppose in a way you don't want the baby and on the other hand maybe you do want the baby. So it would be kind of a sad thing to think you'd lose the baby, even though you might also have the feeling that you wouldn't want the baby.

TA: I wanted it before. But I don't now.

DR: You don't now. Maybe it's kind of because you're preparing yourself in case you lose it. . . . What does your boy friend think about the fact that you're going to have a baby? What does he say about that?

TA: He wanted to marry me, but his mom won't let him.

DR: What does your mother say?

TA: Oh, it's her own fault. She can't say nothin to me.

DR: She can't—how's that?

TA: Oh, all the time, we go out—she don't care what time we come in—she don't care about NOTHING, not nothing. We come in at four or five o'clock and she doesn't say nothin.

DR: Has it always been that way, Mary?

TA: As far back as I can remember. She doesn't care about us. All she does is give us food and a place to sleep. That's all she says she has to do by law—give us food and a place to sleep.

DR: And she said that? Sounds like she's kind of angry with you, too.

TA: She said that a long time ago—she says it all the time. She used to beat us and everything. She don't do it now—if she did it now—she don't do it now cause we ran away, me and Joan. We ran away I—and I guess she needed someone to do all her work for her, or something, that's why she's so good—she said, I'll be good to you. She doesn't hit us now. I don't do none of her work either. I live in a house by myself and all the time she tells me she wants me to clean the house in front. And she's so junky. She buys a bunch of junk, you know, and she throws it all over the house. She buys things she don't need. She buys toys for Ben, from the second hand store or somethin, and they're so broken up. She could of bought maybe one or two good toys with it, but instead she buys millions and millions of junky toys. That's the way she is. Just a junk collector. You should see the yard. It's like a pig pen. I'm embarrassed to bring anyone there. She gave me the house out back, the house we used to live in before she built the house in front. And I go back there—my grandmother used to live in it, but my grand-mother died last February or March—and—and I keep that place real clean, you know, and that's where I bring every-body to go out to. I hate people to come to my house and have to walk through the front house, and see all of that junk . . . She don't care.

DR: Where's your father?

TA: He left me when I was just a baby. I don't blame him—my mom, she thinks she can rule everybody—tell them what to do, you know?

DR: Why did he leave?

TA: I don't know. I had a picture of him once, and my mom, she saw me with it and ripped it up. She said, you don't need that— she wouldn't let me keep it.

DR: And she's never remarried?

TA: Yeah—she's had lots of husbands. She's been married seven times.

DR: Since your father?

TA: No—three—four times since my dad.

DR: So your youngest brother then is . . .

TA: . . . adopted.

DR: Oh, he's adopted!

TA: She don't tell no one that he's adopted—she wants them to believe that she had him.

DR: Why did she want to adopt another child when she already had a lot of children?

TA: I don't know.

DR: How long ago did she adopt him?

TA: When he was just a little baby.

DR: About three years ago?

TA: When I was in the 6th grade—I was 12, I think.

DR: It sounds to me, Mary, like Sue is rather close to you—or Joan is rather close to you. You're closer to her perhaps than the others?—or are you?

TA: I guess I am.

DR: Why are you so close to Joan? Because she's closer to your age?

TA: I don't know. All my brothers and sisters—well, my two oldest brothers—Dan, he's never lived with us—he's always lived with his dad. And then Frank, as soon as he, he [sic] went in the Army as soon as he could, to get away from Mom. And then John went into the service as soon as he could. And Mary Ann, I don't know, I used to be real close to her but then she, then she got, she went around with Sam for 5 years and after she started "steadying" with him and I just never have nothing to do with her now. And Earl's around, and she's, ever since then she's been, I don't know, real mean, and, and, nothin, you know?

DR: Does she still live at home? And Joan, how old is she?

TA: 17. She'll be 18 December 8th . . .

DR: What do you think about the fact that Joan does use marijuana?

TA: If she wants to do it, let her do it.

DR: Does it make you feel badly, because she does it?

TA: It used to—I don't care now. I don't care about no one. No one cares about me.

DR: No one at all?

TA: Earl does, I guess.

DR: That's your boy friend? . . . What are you going to do about this idea of marriage? Is anything going to come of it?

TA: No.

DR: Would you like to get married with him?

TA: I did—I don't now.

DR: Why do you feel that you don't?

TA: He broke up with me. And then just because I took the pills—he found out about it, well, he says, here take my rings back, you know? He was just doing it, you know, cause I did that . . . [attempted suicide]

DR: Joan, when you—Mary, when you previously made the suicide attempts, what did you do at that time, what did you use?

TA: I just took a bottle of aspirins, and then I got so sick I vomited them up all over.

DR: Both times? Was there anybody around when you took them?

TA: No. This is the first time anyone's been around.

DR: And did they know that you took them this time?

TA: Yeah. Glen saw the three bottles sittin there. And he said, what's this?—cause he knew me and Earl'd got in a fight—and he likes me, or sumpin, I don't know. He's been in jail and just got out.

DR: Glen is who?

TA: He's just a friend of Earl's.

DR: He's Earl's friend?

TA: Yeah. And he likes me, and he come in and he saw the bottles and he knew we'd got in a big fight, and he said, what's this? And I said, well I don't know—look at it—it's bottles. (laughs) Then he said, you took em, huh? And I said, you think I'd tell you if I did take them? And he said, no. And I said, well I'm not going to tell you. And he said, oh thank you. He knew I'd took em, so then he just sat there, and you know he—he told me that—that he'd marry me, and he said—and he told me, even if you don't care about me, a little, even if you don't care about me, he says, I'll pay for it and everything, and . . .

DR: Pay for the baby?

TA: Yeah, cause Earl's parents won't let him marry me, you know. And so then he took—he started drinking—and it was crazy—we just sat there, and then I asked him to take me over to Earl's house. And I went over to Earl's and talked to him, and then his dad came in that night.

DR: This is after you'd taken the pills?

TA: Yeah, and I went there, and I talked to him and he took me home, but when I got home, well, Glen had went home before, cause I don't know—I fell asleep over at Earl's and they kept trying to wake me; they was shaking me, and I could feel them shaking me, but I just couldn't—couldn't wake up I guess. I don't know, I was just layin there. (Laughs) Finally, I got up and Glen went home, and when Earl was taking me, they'd told my mom, so when I got home, Mom was there, and then cops came a little while later, and they talked to me, and they went through the house trying to find something.

DR: Who was it who really told?—was it Glen?—he told your mother?

TA: He told my mom.

DR: And she in turn called the police? . . . You know, when people do this sort of thing, especially when teen-agers do this, it's usually because they want help . . . What do you think about that?

TA: I don't know. I don't need no one to help me.

DR: I guess everyone needs someone—we all sometimes get the feeling that we can get along without anybody because we've had to get along by ourselves so much. But I guess we all need somebody. I think that's why you smiled when you were talking about Glen, because it meant something for you to have him say to you, well I'll take care of the baby and I'll take care of you.

TA: Well, it does sort of.

DR: It made you feel good inside to think that somebody cared enough to do that, even though you might not love him. Isn't that really the way it felt? . . . Sure! . . . I think it's important for people—everybody needs somebody to care for them. Just as you needed it—and it makes you feel very sad, so sad that you wonder what's the purpose of going on if people don't care for you.

TA: There's nothin left . . . Why do they have me stay here so long?

DR: Well, we want to do more tests, Mary. We want to do some psychological testing, and Dr. W_____ will be seeing you and I'll see you for probably at least one more visit. And then I'd like to be able to see you after you leave here—for you to come in and see me about once a week perhaps? This will be up to you to decide—if you want to come in and see me . . .

TA: I have someone that comes to my mind.

DR: Who? Who did you have in mind?

TA: I don't know how I am with Earl cause of that [the suicide attempt]. Can he come see me?

DR: Well your mother can see you dear. But Earl, I would have to say no, at this point.

TA: I don't want to see her! Just never mind at all. I don't want to see her. I don't want to.

DR: It's perfectly all right for her to come, but I'd prefer that Earl, under the circumstances . . .

TA: Why?

DR: How old—how old is Earl?

TA: Sixteen.

DR: How does your mother feel about the fact that you're pregnant and that Earl is responsible for it? What does she say?

TA: She's trying to get rid of me. She wants me to marry him. She just wants me to get away so she don't have to support me.

DR: What did she say about the baby?

TA: Oh, she thinks she's gonna get it. Well, she's full of it, man. She ain't gonna touch that kid—she ain't gonna beat it—mistreat it. It ain't gonna live like I lived!

DR: What does your mother do for an income? How does she get along.

TA: Cooking—our stepdad—he's a cook.

DR: Oh, he's a cook, too. Does your stepfather live in the home?

TA: Yes.

DR: How do you get along with him?

TA: I don't like him.

DR: Why?

TA: I just don't like him. He bugs me. He hit me once. And I hate him. He—he—we have these cars you know, and he's been drunk, you know, and he had em in an accident twice now, you know. And he's messed the cars up real bad, and Mom and everybody lost their insurance, cause he was on the insurance thing. And just messed up a lot of money. And then he had Mom build that house and it took a lot of money, and now all the time she bugs us about having to put money out on us. We don't use none of her money. She hasn't bought me any clothes in a year and a half. She hasn't bought me anything. Me and Joan—me and Joan, we—we go out, you know, we go out every once in a while we go out and steal clothes from the store. (Laughs) Cause we don't got nothin to wear. Or, I have to earn my own money; I iron clothes for this guy—really for a whole family—she has 8 kids, and Bobby he lives there now, he's 22 or 23. And I iron his clothes for him every week, you know, when like he washes them and they have to be ironed. He's separated from his wife. And I get money like that. Or I used to iron for Mary Ann, but she doesn't have any ironing any more. I used to clean this guy's apartment every week— that's the only way I got money was to get it for myself.

DR: And you always got it yourself?

TA: Yeah, I had to go earn it myself. Cause Mom, she begrudged me every little penny I got. One night I asked her for 6 cents— I don't know what I wanted to buy, but I needed 6 cents. She says, I don't got it. Six cents!—she had it—she just didn't want to give it to me.

DR: Do you go to school?

TA: Yeah.

DR: Where do you go to school?

TA: Lakeview High School.

DR: What grade are you in?

TA: Tenth.

DR: How do you do in school?—how have you been doing in school?

TA: I used to do real good in school. This year I don't do nothin.

DR: When you say real good—what kind of grades did you get?

TA: I used to get—average—B. I used to . . . every once in a while I'd go as low as a C, and I might get an A. But I was usually just a B student.

DR: That's a pretty good student. B student is better than average.

TA: And this year, now I'm failing.

DR: What do you think was the reason that you've been failing this year?

TA: I don't know.

DR: Is it since you went back to school this time?

TA: Yeah.

DR: What do you think might be the reason that you're having difficulty?

TA: I just don't know . . . It bores me. . . .

DR: Do the kids know that you're pregnant?

TA: No. And I don't care if they do or not. It's none of their business!

DR: Mary, who is your closest friend? . . . Or do you have a close friend that you can talk to?

TA: No.

DR: No one at all?

TA: The only one I talk to is Earl.

DR: How about Joan?

TA: I wouldn't talk to her. She don't even know—nobody knows but my mom . . .

DR: She doesn't even know you're pregnant?

TA: Just my mom and my stepdad, Earl and his mom and dad and his sister and grandma and aunt. There's no one in my family knows—except my mom and stepdad.

DR: You said you were close to Joan—but I guess you're not that close, close enough to have confidences together. Not that close. Do you have any girl friends that you're very close to?

TA: I never had— I don't know, just in school. I never went to see them. I don't have anybody real close to me.

DR: Have you had difficulty in making friends, Mary?

TA: No! I have a lot of friends, it's just that I . . .

DR: Have you always had a lot of friends?

TA: It's just that I don't stay with any one. I mean, I don't get too close or involved with anyone, cause when you lose a friend, you know, it hurts awful bad. And so I just don't get involved with anybody. I just sort of—make the rounds and have a lot of friends.

DR: What do you do for your own enjoyment? What sort of things do you enjoy doing, that you do?

TA: I love to go riding.

DR: Riding? Horseback?

TA: Unhuh, but the horse hasn't been rode about a year and a half now, and Mom won't put shoes on it, and Mom won't, I don't know, she got real mad one time, and she said, oh don't you just touch my horse. So I don't touch him. I don't feed him. I don't water him. I don't do nothin. She sold my horse once— she didn't even tell me. She just took it to the auction and she sold it. And I asked her, I said, where's Flicka? And she said, oh I sold her. And I said, what? And she said, I sold her. She didn't care. And I'd bought the horse.

DR: You did buy it? How long ago was that? . . .

TA: (Crying) Oh, about two years ago.

DR: How long had you had the horse?

TA: About three years.

DR: So you were quite close by then. You must have liked the horse quite a bit.

TA: Yeah. She wasn't a very good horse though. She had a ring bone—she limped, you know. You couldn't ride her very long. She limped—she had to rest.

DR: I'm surprised anybody would buy her.

TA: She was a real good horse for kids. All the kids used to love to ride her. She was, you know, real gentle and all that. She was a good horse—she just loved kids.

DR: I bet you loved her, too . . . What other things do you like to do besides ride?

TA: I like to read.

DR: What do you usually read?

TA: I like mysteries a lot.

DR: —like James Bond?

TA: I don't know. Just—

DR: Just any kind?

TA: About people gettin killed, or lost treasures, or you know just any kind of mystery that leaves you wondering . . . I like to read those true confession love stories, you know—they're interestin.

DR: What do you like most about them?

TA: I don't know. (Laughs) Reading about other people—what happened to them—what they do . . .

DR: What other things do you do with your spare time—when you're not in school?

TA: I like to go to the beach. I love the beach.

DR: Do you surf?

TA: I used to. I don't any more.

DR: Why, because of the baby?

TA: No. I never knew how to swim, but I used to go out there and surf and all. Whenever I was gonna fall off I'd just jump to the side and grab ahold of the board you know. And then, I don't know—I got scared. I almost drowned one time, and I haven't been out since. I should go out there—I'm going to go out soon as I learn how to swim—ain't nothin going to throw me and me not get back on. I used to have a horse that used to do that—she was an Arabian. She used to throw me every day, five or six times, and I'd get right back on her! (Laughs)

DR: What would she do? Did you ever wear her out? Did you finally wear her down?

TA: No—both of us would be weared out—I kept gettin back on her though.

DR: Did you ever finally ride her?

TA: Yeah.

DR: How come your mother has horses?

TA: I don't know—she loves animals. We used to have six dogs, and—she—she brings anything stray home you know, just anything. She don't care.

DR: Well horses aren't stray—a horse isn't.

TA: No. But she does things for people. She don't got the money. She don't got the time. She does things, but she never gets it done—she never finishes it, you know? Just crazy. I finally— we got rid of the dog. I had this dog, Bimbo, and she gave it to the dog pound about a week—maybe two weeks ago. You know, she was going to have puppies. It was her fourth or fifth litter. I'd had her since she was a little bitty puppy about three days old—not that little. But just a itty-bitty thing—just after it was born—it wasn't even weaned yet. I fed it out of a bottle for a long time. And, and I saved money so I could get her spayed, you know, cause I—Mom didn't like having her around havin puppies. And so I had the money, and then one day— Mom never did it—then she said she had to use the money for sumpin else. So I gave her away to the dogpound so they could put her to sleep—cause it was real hard on her to have pups.

DR: She'd had them once?

TA: Yeah. It was about the fourth or fifth litter when I gave her away. She was pregnant, she was going to have pups. But when she had them she usually had about 10 or 12, and I didn't want any more cause it hurt her and so I decided to give her away—told them to put her to sleep.

DR: When you and your mother have talks, do—do you ever have talks?

TA: I never talk to my mother.

DR: You never talk to her?

TA: I've never talked to her. You know how kids—you know, girls—they can be real close to their mom and they confide in her and everything—I never talked to my mom. The only reason I told her that I was like this was—was—I don't know, I guess cause I realized I needed doctor's care. That's the only reason.

DR: Maybe you thought it would upset her, too.

TA: Well, so what. I wish I'd hurt her so bad it'd kill her.

DR: I guess she didn't show much concern?

TA: All the time she's buggin me.

DR: Do you ever talk to your stepfather?

TA: I never talk to him. He don't know nothin. He's stupid. He thinks he knows everything He thinks he knows—he thinks he's the best cook in the world. He thinks he knows about everything and anything, and he's so stupid he don't know nothin. He brags about nothin. He says he's been all over the United States—he says everywhere in the world. And I go, Yah Yah. He says he can cook the best—you know if he doesn't like a cook on the job where he works, if he doesn't like one of the guys workin there, he quits—he just quits, up and leaves, cause he don't like a person. He thinks he's so—good, or somethin.

DR: Does your mother drink?—you said that your father, or your stepfather—

TA: No. Mom doesn't drink, smoke—but she sure makes up for it with cussin.

DR: She cusses a lot? What does she cuss about?

TA: You know—when she gets mad at us—she just lets out. You know I never said nothin against her—you know—I've never, until maybe about six months ago. And then, you know, I'd said it to myself, before I've never said anything wrong against my mom. I just stood her. I didn't even think anything about her. I just thought, well, so what, just let her blow up. Oh, she makes me mad now. I call her anything I can think of . . . I get mad.

DR: You said you had several other stepfathers—were you close to any of them?

TA: No.

DR: Why was that, Mary?

TA: (Sighs) I don't know. They were all—Joe, this one—I don't know, they were always so mean, and then this one, Gordon, he used to beat me with a belt. And, I don't know, they were all mean. They weren't nothin. They . . .

DR: Were you ever told anything about your own father?

TA: No. My mom acts like he don't even exist. I ask her about him—she don't say nothin.

DR: Do you know that he is alive?—or where he is?

TA: I don't know whether he is or not.

DR: You don't know where he is? . . .

TA: I guess that he's alive . . .

DR: Mary, what do you think—say, if you were allowed to leave the hospital—this is just for example, but if you were allowed to leave the hospital today, what do you think you might do about suicide?

TA: Well, I wouldn't do it no more.

DR: Why do you say that?

TA: I just—I don't know—I just wouldn't.

DR: Now you've made three attempts, and I wonder why you feel so strongly that you wouldn't do it again?

TA: Cause I wouldn't. I don't know why.

DR: You mean because you were so sick? Usually there's some kind of reason . . .

TA: I don't know if I would or not.

DR: You're not sure then?

TA: No.

DR: If things got bad you might try it again? . . . If Earl didn't make up with you again—what would you think?

TA: Oh, he made up with me that night. He just made up with me cause I took those pills. I don't know what he'll . . .

DR: You don't know what he'll do, hmm? . . .

TA: Can't I see him any time I'm in here?

DR: You'll only be in here a few days.

TA: Well that's a long time—with nothin to do.

DR: We'll try to find things to keep you busy. I think you'll find some people on the ward that you'll find you'll have a chance to talk with, and you'll have a chance to talk with other teenagers. There are other people your age on the ward. There are no adults and no young children on the ward—just teenagers— 14 through 17 years of age. So there's going to be somebody perhaps that you'll have a chance to talk with . . . Do you have any questions you'd like to ask me at this point?

TA: Do you just think I'm crazy or somethin?

DR: No. I don't think you're crazy. Do you think you are?

TA: No. I ain't crazy.

DR: We don't think you're crazy either, but we think it's pretty important when somebody tries to take their own life. It usually means they're pretty upset about something. And most often it means that they'd like some kind of help . . . And that's what we're here to do, is try to understand what's been going on and why it is that you haven't been able to talk about it.

THE USE OF SUICIDE NOTES AS A SOURCE OF DATA

Another valuable source of data were the suicide notes of the adolescent suicide attempters. Four notes were actually collected. The accounts of three others were related to me by the suicide attempters and their parents.

These were used in two ways; firstly, the data from the content of the note was incorporated into the case history accounts in order to make them as complete as possible, and secondly, they were analyzed in their own right out of the context of the particular case history. The factual information acquired from the notes was incorporated into the analysis of the data found in the first part of Chapter 3. The latter part of Chapter 3 concerns itself with the second way in which the notes were used, i.e. *to delineate the "internal" process by which the adolescent overcame the moral constraints against suicide and thus bridged the gap between thought and action.*

While I relied primarily upon the case history data for the answers to the questions, "What non-shareable problems do the suicide attempters have?", or "What was it they experienced which led to their progressive isolation from meaningful social relationships?", I relied primarily upon the notes in attempting to find the answer to "What verbalizations did they apply to their intended act that allowed them to adjust their conception of themselves as trusted persons with their behavior as trust violators?" An analysis of suicide notes left by the suicide attempters in this study, as well as by adolescents successful in suicide and not a part of this study, revealed a common process at work. A discussion of the formal aspects of this process will also be presented toward the end of Chapter 3.

FOOTNOTES

1. Donald R. Cressey, *Other People's Money* (Glencoe, Illinois: Free Press, 1953), p. 12.

2. *Ibid.,* p. 30.

3. *Ibid.,* p. 16.

4. Adolescent Suicide Attempts Project, funded by a National Institute of Mental Health Grant, Research #R11MH01432–02, Co-Directed by Jerry Jacobs, Ph.D. and Joseph D. Teicher, M.D.

5. The position of the parents in each of these cases was that they had no intention of allowing their child to participate in the study. Their children were withdrawn from the hospital as soon as possible—in two cases against medical advice. In addition, it was made perfectly clear that "the less said about the attempt, the better."

CHAPTER 3

Finding and Interpretation of Data

A common denominator to the life histories of the adolescent suicide attempters was not found in some isolated or independent event. *What I have attempted to delineate were the formal aspects of a process through which the adolescent had to progress in order to, first, entertain, and then, attempt suicide.* My general approach was social-psychological. I felt it was necessary to undertake at least two basic considerations in describing such a process: 1) the formal aspects of the chronological ordering of sets of events in the everyday life of the adolescent, and 2) how the adolescent experienced these events and reacted to them.

The necessity for an evaluation of the second step is based on a key assumption of psychiatry and psychology, that two persons subject to the same event can "experience" it differently, and that one's behavior is based ultimately upon the "experience" and not the event. There stems from this contention the necessity of allowing for "personal differences." Granted, there is a range of occurrences in which the same event may be viewed and experienced differently by different persons. It is also true that there are many events which persons in like situations tend to view and experience in the same way. For example, 40 per cent of the adolescent suicide attempters had stepparents, usually stepfathers, and in every case the stepparent was seen by the adolescent as unwanted. The separation of parents, broken romances, residential moves, and unanticipated school changes, were, without exception, viewed as unwelcome events. One might argue that there is no natural necessity involved in the above consensus, e.g. the adolescent might love his stepparent, feel he is well rid of a sweetheart, or move to a preferred neighborhood. However, this was not true of the adolescents studied.

Making allowances for "individual differences" to prove the exception, the rule seems to be, with respect to the events listed above and those considered in Table B in the appendix, that they were all experienced as unwelcome and resulted in the adolescent's unhappiness. If a series of these events occur in the particular sequence outlined earlier in the author's

63

Central Hypothesis, they seem to result in the adolescent's experiencing extreme unhappiness and withdrawal. Why should this be? *It is postulated that these events (or comparable ones) experienced by the adolescent in the right sequence will lead to his progressive unhappiness because they have led to his progressive isolation from meaningful social relationships. This isolation, in turn, is seen by the adolescent as "the problem" and simultaneously serves to isolate him from that segment of the population necessary to help him resolve the problem, i.e. help him to reestablish meaningful relationships.*

Keeping in mind that certain events may be experienced in the same way by different persons and that these events seem to result in the adolescent's progressive unhappiness—a state he projects into a pessimistic future world view—the central concern of this study was to compare the presence or absence and chronological ordering of these sets of events in the life histories of fifty adolescent suicide attempters with those found in the life histories of thirty-one control adolescents matched on age, race, sex, and level of mother's education.

The process which led to the adolescent suicide attempters' progressive isolation from significant others and, finally, to the suicide attempt, is described below. The reader will recognize this process as the first four points of the outline noted earlier on pages 27–28.

1. A long-standing history of problems (from childhood to the onset of adolescence).
2. A period of "escalation of problems" (since the onset of adolescence and in excess of those "normally" associated with adolescence).
3. The progressive failure of available adaptive techniques for coping with old and increasing new problems which leads the adolescent to a progressive social isolation from meaningful social relationships.
4. The final phase, characterized by the chain reaction dissolution of any remaining meaningful social relationships in the weeks and days preceding the suicide attempt.

The fifth point (the internal process by which the individual justifies his intended suicide to himself) will be discussed in some detail later in this chapter. It will also be shown that the thirty-one adolescents of the control group were not subject to this process.

Arranging the events in the adolescent's life in chronological order proved a distinct advantage. From this perspective, any particular event (e.g. broken homes) or set of events was not viewed in isolation, but with respect to when it occurred and/or reoccurred within the context of the life history.

Context gave any particular occurrence its significance. It was the lack of attention paid to the ordering and context of events that led Durkheim, Stengel and others to conclude that no event was so insignificant that it could not suffice, depending upon one's "proneness," to lead one to suicide.

The analysis of data will be divided into the four stages cited above. An analysis will be made from two perspectives, i.e. group data and matched pairs. Tables C and D in the Appendix will allow the reader to view the distribution of selected events in the life history of any one of the thirty-one cases of matched pairs. Table B presents the group data derived from Tables C, D and E for the first and second stages of the four stage process described on the preceding page. The fourth stage will be considered separately on pages 67–68. The discussion of stages one, two and four, therefore, will rest upon an analysis of the data found in Tables B, C, D, and E. An analysis of the data for the remaining non-matched nineteen cases of suicide attempters in these time periods, not considered in the matched pair analysis, is also considered separately in these tables.

Following this will be a discussion of the failure of adaptive techniques (stage three), experienced by the suicide attempters in dealing with these events. Table 1, page 69 presents the numbers of adolescents involved and kinds of "behavioral problems" experienced. This is followed by a discussion of the chronological ordering of "behavioral problems," viewed here as "adaptive techniques," that the suicide attempters and control adolescents have experienced. This will be considered with respect to the measures taken by the parents (disciplinary techniques) to counter these "behavioral problems" (see Table H in the Appendix), i.e. the way the parents unintentionally set about systematically eliminating the adaptive techniques available to the adolescent, and how this process led to a feeling on the part of the suicide attempters that a suicide attempt was "the only way out."

A COMPARISON OF THE NATURE, NUMBER AND SEQUENCE OF EVENTS IN THE LIVES OF THE SUICIDE ATTEMPTERS AND CONTROL ADOLESCENTS

In perusing the above thesis, the key question arises whether or not the adolescent suicide attempters experienced any set of events in some particular order that the control adolescents did not. Table B presents the total number of experiences and the total number of persons experiencing them for twenty-one categories of social-structural events in the life histories of thirty-one matched pairs of suicide attempters and control adolescents. These 21 categories of social-structural events were selected on the basis of an earlier analysis of the most significant events in the life histories of the forty-eight adolescents that comprised the pre-test group previously noted on page 28. The table is given in two time periods, i.e. from birth through 1958, and from 1959 until the time of the interview. The beginning of the latter stage represents, roughly, the onset of adolescence. Also presented in Table B is the same data for nineteen non-matched cases of suicide attempters.

The reader will note the intentional omission of individual statistical analysis for each of the twenty-one categories. It is important to remember that it was not a particular incident in the adolescents' lives that led them to attempt suicide; the nature, number, and ordering of events were the crucial factors. Our analysis will consequently be concerned primarily with these factors.

How did the events in the life histories of the suicide attempters and control adolescents compare with each other? Analysis of these two tables reveals the following. Whereas the suicide attempters were generally subject to a greater number of debilitating events a greater number of times, the differentials between the two were much smaller in the first period than in the second. This finding has two important features. Not only were the suicide attempters subject to a more extensive and intensive "long standing history of problems" than the control adolescents (38 per cent of the suicide attempters and 94 per cent of the control adolescents characterized their childhood as being "happy"), but for the suicide attempters these original problems did not tend to diminish in the second period. At the same time that old problems were extended or reappeared, new ones were added. This was not true of the life histories of the control adolescents. *The result for the suicide attempters was an abrupt escalation of problems coinciding with the onset of adolescence.*

For example, Table B indicates, with respect to the total number of residential moves and school changes, and the number of adolescents subject to them, that there was a relatively small differential between the suicide attempters and control group in the first time period. Of the thirty-one matched pairs, only four suicide attempters and seven control adolescents had no residential or school changes in the first time period, i.e. both groups experienced a considerable amount of residential mobility and school change. (See Table C) However, the differential on these two items in the second period is much larger. In fact, only two suicide attempters out of thirty-one matched pairs had not experienced a residential move or school change, whereas thirteen out of thirty-one control adolescents had no residential moves or school changes in this period. It is clear that whereas both groups had, early in life, experienced considerable disruption with respect to the above variables, from adolescence on, the control group had benefited from a stabilizing effect that the suicide attempters had not.

The escalation of problems among the suicide attempters is graphically

illustrated in other areas as well. In the first period, twelve suicide attempters and seven control adolescents experienced a broken home, i.e. the loss
of at least one parent through death, separation or divorce. In the second
time period, fourteen suicide attempters and only two control adolescents
were subject to the devastating effects of this event. Furthermore, for most
of the suicide attempters this event constituted a reoccurring theme. The
same was true for "parents remarrying." Here again we see that in the first
period the parents of five suicide attempters and four control adolescents
remarried. In the second time period the parents of nine suicide attempters
and only one control adolescent had remarried. Then too, four suicide
attempters and two control adolescents in the first period had experienced
having to live with relatives for extended periods of time in the absence of
both parents. In the second time period, nine suicide attempters and two
control adolescents had this experience. The problem of "heavy drinking"
in the family was nearly the same for the experimental and control groups
of adolescents in the first time period. Once again, we find that in the second time period it has diminished for the control adolescents and increased
for the attempters. Suicide attempts by friends, relatives, parents, or the
adolescent himself are practically non-existent for both groups in the first
period. In the second time period, the parents of three suicide attempters
had made a total of ten suicide attempts; in eight cases, ten friends or relatives of the suicide attempters made a suicide attempt, and the suicide
attempters themselves had in thirteen cases made a total of twenty prior
suicide attempts. There were no suicide attempts in any of these categories
for the control adolescents, their parents or friends.

For further examples of this trend of a progressive social isolation the
reader has only to examine Tables B, C, D, and E. It becomes apparent
that the life histories of the suicide attempters adhered to stages one and
two, i.e. "a long standing history of problems" and an "escalation" of problems during adolescence above and beyond those usually associated with
this period. It is equally clear that the adolescents in the control group were
much less subject to the events characterizing these two stages.

What of the fourth stage—the feeling on the part of the adolescent that
he was subject to a complete disintegration of meaningful social relationships in the weeks and months immediately preceding the attempt? Several
of the events listed in Tables B, C, D and E occurred very often immediately prior to the attempt. For example, among the matched pairs, ten suicide attempters and zero control adolescents were not enrolled in school.
A total of thirteen suicide attempters and seven control adolescents had a
serious romance in progress immediately preceding the interview. Eight of
these thirteen romances had terminated for the suicide attempters, while all
of those of the control adolescents were ongoing. Three suicide attempters

of the matched pairs (five others of the non-matched pairs) were pregnant or believed themselves pregnant at the time of the attempt, whereas none of the control adolescents had this experience. Ten suicide attempters and zero control adolescents were institutionalized, i.e. sent to Juvenile Hall or jail during this period. Ten suicide attempters and two control adolescents had experienced a serious physical illness or injury within the last year or so. Eight suicide attempters and only two control adolescents had been hospitalized late in the second period or just prior to the attempt.

The effects on the adolescent of being sent to Juvenile Hall, experiencing a serious physical illness, being hospitalized, dropping out or being suspended from school, having a romance culminate abruptly, and/or discovering pregnancy, all lead to the isolation of the adolescent from meaningful social relationships. The same was true of all the events cited in the first and second time periods. These separations occurred abruptly and unexpectedly. Any and all of them were serious even when experienced as independent events. But we must remember that they did not occur in isolation but within the context of all that was previously discussed. Consequently, the suicide attempter had not only experienced a greater number of disruptive events a greater number of times, but these problems tended to escalate. The set of events to which they were subject was also more serious in nature. I do not propose here to offer an exact weighting scheme for the categories given in Table B. However, it must be clear that the loss of a parent on one occasion is not, for example, comparable to one residential move. In short, to appreciate the seriousness of the adolescent suicide attempter's predicament at the time of the attempt, we must consider the number of events, their frequency, the nature of the events and the sequence in which they occurred. In doing so, we find in this calculus of despair that what is most important is not any particular event, but the extent to which the suicide attempters were subject to a set of events in a particular order, the sum of which constituted a process of progressive social isolation.

"BEHAVIORAL PROBLEMS"

In order to better delineate the features of this process, I will consider next the onset of "behavioral problems" and their reciprocal effects upon the adolescents and their parents. This discussion will be pursued from four different points of view: 1) the number of behavioral problems, 2) the kinds of behavioral problems, 3) the discrepancy in perception between the adolescent and parent regarding "behavioral problems" and finally, 4) under "adaptive" vs. "maladaptive" techniques, the sequential ordering of "behavioral problems."

The first question to be considered is whether or not there was a significant difference in the number of "behavioral problems" experienced by the suicide attempters and control adolescents since the onset of the "escalation period." Using a Mann Whitney–U Test, a rank ordering by number of behavioral problems for the experimental and control groups reveals an average difference in ranks significant at the .001 level. (See Table F, in the Appendix.)

Grouping "behavioral problems" (viewed here as "adaptive techniques") into three categories, "Rebellion," "Withdrawal into Self" and "Physical Withdrawal," Table 1 which follows presents the kinds of behaviors associated with each of the three categories and the per cent of adolescents from each group who experienced them. The eight items included in the three categories of "Adaptive Techniques" were chosen from a list of seventeen behavioral items and an "other" on the basis of the answers given by the forty-eight adolescents comprising the pre-test group previously noted. These adolescents were not a part of the study sample. The adolescents in the pre-test group most frequently referred to the above eight behaviors as ways in which they tried unsuccessfully to bring their problems to the

Table 1

"Behavioral Problems" Since 1959
Viewed as "Adaptive Techniques"

			Experimental Group (N = 31)		Control Group (N = 31)		Unmatched Experimental (N = 19)	
			%	N	%	N	%	N
I.	REBELLION							
	Disobedience		48	(15)	31	(10)	42	(8)
	Sassiness		48	(15)	47	(15)	79	(15)
	Defiance		19	(6)	25	(8)	37	(7)
	Rebelliousness		29	(9)	6	(2)	31	(6)
II.	WITHDRAWAL INTO SELF							
	Gloominess	*	57	(17)	13	(4)	60	(12)
	Won't Talk	a.	40	(12)	19	(6)	47	(9)
	Withdrawn	†	43	(13)	3	(1)	70	(14)
III.	PHYSICAL WITHDRAWAL							
	Running Away from Home	†	43	(13)	3	(1)	58	(11)

*X^2 for matched groups significant at the .01 level (one-tailed)
†X^2 for matched groups significant at the .001 level (one-tailed)
NOTE: X^2 with Yates correction was computed for the matched pairs of the experimental and control groups only. The data from the unmatched experimental group tended to support the chi squares for the matched pairs.
a.$P < 15$, but Gamma$=.449$ indicating a relatively strong relationship.

attention of their parents. The actual items comprising each of the three categories were selected by the author as being most representative of those categories. The author's choice was independently validated by the project's research assistant. The reason for viewing these items both as "behavioral problems" and "adaptive techniques" will be discussed more fully on following pages.

The seventeen behavioral items (or "other") were also derived from the pre-testing of the first draft of the interview schedule which indicated these seventeen items to be most frequently mentioned by the adolescent and parents as "behavior problems." The "other" category was to allow for any additional behavioral problems not anticipated by the seventeen items cited above. It should be noted that the parents and adolescents resorted to the category of "other" only infrequently. In short, the subjects' evaluation of the seventeen items above seems to have been, for all intents and purposes, an exhaustive set with respect to "behavioral problems."

The table reveals that in general both the suicide attempters and control adolescents had resorted to behaviors associated with the "Rebellion" category. However, few of the control adolescents and a high percentage of suicide attempters had enlisted behaviors in the "Withdrawal into Self" and "Physical Withdrawal" categories as a means of coping with their problems. This finding is important in light of the fact that the latter techniques are indicative of a later stage of development in the process leading up to the suicide attempt. Adolescent behavior characterized by "won't talk," "withdrawn" etc., the sum of which is generally taken to constitute a "flattening of affect," is generally indicative of the advanced stages of the adolescent's alienation from his parents and others. One statistical indication of the extent of this alienation is the fact that although 70 per cent of all the suicide attempts took place in the home, often with the parent in the next room, only *20 per cent* of those who reported their attempt, reported it to their parents. It was not uncommon to find the adolescent calling his friend who lived miles away, who in turn called the parents sitting in the next room to inform them of the attempt.

Another interesting finding with respect to the number of "behavioral problems" the adolescents experienced during the escalation stage was that the suicide attempters experienced the onset of a 50 per cent greater number of behavioral problems during this period than did the control adolescents.

What of the discrepancies in perception between the adolescent and parents regarding "behavioral problems?" Did the adolescents and their parents generally agree on which "behavioral problems" were at issue? The average per cent of difference in perception with respect to *how many* "behavioral problems" existed was small for both groups (suicide attempters, 10 per cent; control adolescents, 5 per cent). However, the average per cent of difference in perception between the adolescent and parent with regard to *which* behavioral problems existed was considerable in both groups, i.e. 30 per cent for the suicide attempters and 27 per cent for the control group.

Are these statistics in any way indicative of adolescent-parent interpersonal relationships? We believe they are. To the extent that adolescent-parent relationships are reciprocally affected by a new set of behaviors originating with adolescence, both the suicide attempters and control group seem to be subject to the same process. However, there was an important distinction to be made—one which puts the suicide attempter at·a distinct disadvantage.

The suicide attempters were forced to contend with nearly 50 per cent more "behavioral problems" during the last five years than the control adolescents of the matched pairs. Since the average per cent of difference in perception between the adolescent and parent in both groups was about 30 per cent with respect to *which* behavioral problems existed, both groups of adolescents felt that they were being disciplined inappropriately about one-third of the time, i.e. disciplined for something they felt they had not done, or not disciplined for something they had done. Because the suicide attempters identified about 50 per cent more "behavioral problems" as having begun in this period, they felt inappropriately disciplined much more often than the control adolescents.

The next aspect to be considered is the way in which the adolescents and their parents tended to view these behaviors. The parents tended to see them exclusively as "behavioral problems," whereas the adolescent saw them both as "behavioral problems" and as "adaptive techniques." The case histories and the data from the transcribed verbatim accounts of the psychiatric interviews indicate that preceding his adoption of these techniques, the adolescent was hopeful that the parent would share his dual perspective and recognize the act—not as just another "misbehavior"—but as an indication that a problem existed. A further expectation was that the parents would view the behavior as a serious effort on his part to bring the problem to their attention through the only means available to him. The entire maneuver by the adolescent was intended to gain access to some source of assistance. In the case of the adolescent suicide attempters, this intended result miscarried. One after another, the teenagers attempted new ways of bringing their problems to the attention of their parents. Having tried all of the above adaptive techniques, they found to their continued frustration that their parents persisted in viewing these acts as new "behavioral problems." In short, there was established and maintained between the adolescent and parent, a lack of a "reciprocity of standpoints and relevances." [1]

By a process of elimination, the field was narrowed to a suicide attempt as an "attention-getting" device and, failing this, suicide was considered.

"DISCIPLINARY TECHNIQUES"

What was the role of "disciplinary techniques" in bringing about the progressive failure of adaptive techniques for the suicide attempters? In pursuing the answer to this question, I will consider first the way in which the adolescents' parents attempted to contend with this new set of behaviors which they took to be "behavioral problems." (See Table H, in the Appendix.) How did the two groups of adolescents compare with respect to (a) the number and kind of disciplinary techniques their parents employed, and (b) the average per cent of difference in perception between adolescent and parent with regard to (a)? As in the case of "behavioral problems," the number of disciplines used in the individual cases were placed in a rank order. The average difference in ranks between the suicide attempters and control adolescents was significant at the .01 level. (See Table G in the Appendix.) According to self-reports, the suicide attempters of the matched pairs were subject to 40 per cent more disciplinary techniques than the adolescents of the control group. The average per cent of difference in perception between the suicide attempters and their parents and the control adolescents and their parents, with respect to *which* disciplines were used, was 55 and 36 per cent respectively. The process described under "behavioral problems," and how the difference in perception worked to escalate the total family conflict, may be applied here as well.

Table F in the Appendix gives an item analysis of the disciplinary techniques used by mothers and fathers of the suicide attempters and control adolescents of the matched pairs. The unmatched sample is considered separately. It is clear here, as in the case of "behavioral problems," that once again the suicide attempters (of the matched and non-matched sets), were at a disadvantage. Whereas the number of parents of suicide attempters using "talking it over" as a technique is only slightly less, and the number using "withholding privileges" only slightly more, *about twice as many parents of suicide attempters as those of the control adolescents used "criticizing," "nagging," "yelling," "withholding approval," or "whipping and spanking."*

What were the reciprocal effects of this process upon the suicide attempters and their parents? Careful analysis of the adolescents' responses to the questions from the structured interview schedules, as well as the transcribed material from the psychiatric interviews reveals that on the one hand, the parents' efforts at reforming the adolescents often seemed inappropriate to the adolescents and were considered to be "nagging"—a form of discipline the study revealed was very frequently used, especially by the mother. On the other hand, the parents' failure to discourage behaviors that the adolescents felt were bad and which they believed they would have been able to overcome with parental help was taken by them as a sign of rejection. The net result from the perspective of the suicide attempters was constant and inappropriate nagging, i.e. unfair discipline and rejection. The net result from the perspective of the parents was increased frustration, which in turn led to their attempting to reduce the dilemma by trying harder. This in turn appeared to the adolescents as either increased nagging and rejection or the inappropriate use by the parents of even more severe disciplinary procedures, i.e., "withholding privileges" is substituted for "nagging" or "criticizing." "Withholding privileges" was the discipline "most often" used by the parents for "most serious" problems and the one considered by the adolescent suicide attempters to be the "worst." As a result, we see again how the suicide attempters were (much more often than the control adolescents) subject to a process of progressive alienation from their parents. Any optimism the parents and teenagers might have initially entertained with respect to converting the other decreased at about the same rate as the level of frustration increased. The result was an uneasy stalemate. It is easy to understand the mutual reluctance of the parents and teenagers to abandon hope of ever "getting through." This reluctance stemmed at least in part from a basic assumption that both the adolescents and parents shared, i.e. that they were rational human beings. "You can tell me, I'll understand," "I was young once too," or for the adolescent, "I'm older than you think," are all expressions which indicate not only an initial willingness to listen but imply the required ability to understand and empathize. To deny the existence of this condition would have necessitated an admission by the adolescents and parents that they were incapable of understanding each other and that all attempts at a meaningful exchange of ideas and any possible resolution of problems by way of this would have been futile. This is, in fact, what ultimately occurred.

Both the adolescents and parents suffered as a result. Table 2 on the following page gives some indication of the extent of the loss from the adolescent's perspective.

Perhaps a more direct indicator of the extent of this alienation is the verbatim accounts of the adolescents themselves.

The following is an example of a fourteen year-old female suicide attempter, taken from the verbatim accounts of the transcribed psychiatric interview.

DR: How often have you run away?
TA: I only ran away once.

Table 2

	Agree or Strongly Agree					
	Matched Pairs				19 Non-matched Pairs	
	Exp. Male N=7 %	Cont. Male N=9 %	Exp. Female N=21 %	Cont. Female N=22 %	Exp. Male N=3 %	Exp. Female N=16 %
(1) "I agree with my parents about what things are important in life."	43 (3)	66 (6)	57 (12)	86 (19)	67 (2)	44 (7)
(2) "It's hard for me to talk to my parents about my problems because they argue."	43 (3)	11 (1)	52 (11)	14 (3)	33 (1)	44 (7)
(3) "When you tell your parents the truth they sometimes punish you."	71 (5)	45 (4)	80 (17)	19 (4)	33 (1)	62 (10)
(4) "When you talk to your parents it's best to be careful what you say."	57 (4)	33 (3)	57 (12)	32 (7)	67 (2)	44 (7)
(5) "I really don't know how to talk to my parents."	29 (2)	0 (0)	57 (12)	28 (6)	67 (2)	69 (11)
(6) "No matter what my problem might be I know my parents will stand behind me."	14 (1)	55 (5)	52 (11)	80 (18)	67 (2)	50 (8)

DR: That was the only time?

TA: No, I did twice.

DR: Twice. Why did you run away?

TA: I don't know. I just seemed to have too many problems with my parents.

DR: So you ran away. But you talked about your sexual experience at that time, you said? Well, did something happen, after you talked about it?

TA: No.

DR: What do you think it is about your parents that you're most angry about?

TA: I don't know. Just when they come home and start yelling at me, for things I didn't do. That's the only time I usually argue with them, is when I get yelled at for something I didn't do.

DR: It's kinda like you can't win with them, huh?

TA: Oh, I can, sometimes. (Laughs) But, I don't know, most of the time I think they win the arguments.

DR: Did your parents know about this other fellow you'd been s— you were having sex with?

TA: Uh-huh.

DR: What'd they say?

TA: I don't know. I didn't talk to them. She never said anything— she didn't mention it to me.

Another by a sixteen year-old boy goes as follows:

DR: What happened?

TA: When? (Laughs)

DR: Well, why you're here.

TA: Well, because I tried to commit suicide.

DR: Why?

TA: Well things weren't going too good at home. Uh, my-uh mother was always yellin at me, and my f—father was always yellin at me and criticizing me all the time. And the kids just wouldn't leave me alone.

DR: Criticizing you?

TA: Yes.

DR: Why?

TA: Well, he said I never did anything right, and that—uh I never had any respect for him, and I was just stupid—and every time I tried to do sumthin I always did it wrong, and so—so what's the use?

Still another reads:

DR: What happened? Tell me about it.
TA: You mean when I took the pills?—and everything?
DR: Yes. Now you took some pills?
TA: Uh-huh. I took 20 aspirins.
DR: 20 aspirin! When did you take them?
TA: I think it was about two or—no, three or four weeks ago, Monday.
DR: 3 or 4 weeks ago on Monday. What time of the day was it?
TA: It was night—at six.
DR: Six o'clock at night. Who was home?
TA: My parents and my younger sister.
DR: And what happened—I mean what happened after you took the pills?
TA: My sister knew that I had some pills in my hands, and she asked where they were, and uh, I just said—well, it's too late now, I've took all of them. And she went to my mother, and right away they rushed me downtown.
DR: And how long were you in the hospital?
TA: A day.
DR: For a day. Was that the first time you ever did that?
TA: Umm-hmm. Yes.
DR: Well, why did you want to do it?
TA: Uh—uh—I guess it was because I was angry at my parents, because they had been arguing, and my mother, a couple of days before, she had been picking on me a lot, and was really mad at me. It was—I think it was, why I did it was to really show them that I—how it hurt me and show them what it could do, you know—all this. That's why I think I did it.
DR: To show them what you could do?
TA: Well, how this—uh—affected me and my sister, how it was hurting us.
DR: Oh, I see. So you had in your mind that by doing this it would be more or less pointing out to your parents what their arguing was—how it was affecting you and your sister?
TA: Yes.

A final entry of a 15 year-old female Mexican-American reads as follows:

DR: I haven't read your record, so you will have to tell me from the beginning how it is you had to come to the hospital.
TA: Oh—(clears throat)

DR: How long have you been here?
TA: Um—four days.
DR: Four days?
TA: Mm-hm.
DR: What happened?
TA: Mm—I was—
DR: I know you must have—well, I know that you must have— well, I know you must have attempted suicide because—
TA: Uh-huh—
DR: —that's why I'm talking to you. So what happened? —what didya do?
TA: It sounds stupid! My mother, she started arguing with me. Cause my father and my—and my mother had gone out. So-uh, they probably went and—I think they—they drank a couple of beers. So when my mother came, she was mad at me. And I didn't know why she was mad at me, cause I was just watchin television. And then—and then she started yellin at me. And then I was wonderin why she was mad at me. So then-uh, I was sposed to have sewn my sister's skirt. And then—and then she told me—I was sewin the—the hem. And so I didn't sew it right. So then my mother started yelling at me, and she said: "You mean that you—uh—you learn sewing at school and you don't even know how to sew!" And then, you know—but she was yellin and everything. And—and then I got mad at her, and then I told her, "At least I'm trying!" And then—my dad, he said, "You don't have to yell at her. Why don't you talk nice to her instead of yellin and everything." And then my mother said, "Why don't you shut up?" And then she told him, "I'm the one that's teaching her." And then my father said, "Well that's not a nice way to teach—to teach them." And so then-uh my mother said-uh—no, my father told my mother, he said, "Is that the way they used to teach you when you were a little girl?" And my mother said, "No. No—nobo—nobody taught me—
DR: Um-hm—
TA: —I had, I had to—I had to do it all by myself."—
DR: Mm-hm—
TA: And then—and then they got mad at one another. And so I— so I went to my room. Then my father said—said-uh, "You stay there and don't—come on out," cause she's just yelling at me and everything. And so then-uh, my mother said, "Come back here! You'd better not go anywhere. Cause I'll slap you

down so hard you won't know what hit you." And then—and then, so then—then my mother told me a bad word, and I told her back. And—

DR: What'd she call you?

TA: I dunno—

DR: Yes you do. What was it?

TA: Huh?

DR: What'd she call you?

TA: Uh, I don't know how to say it.

DR: Well, what does it mean, in your words?

TA: I look-uh fat, or something like that.

DR: Well she called you—something about the way you looked?

TA: Uh-huh! And then I told her, "Well you——!" And then, she got real mad because I said that, and then she said, "You stupid idio—you little rat! What do you think you are—I'm your mother!" And then my dad—he was just there, lookin, he said, "Don't pay attention to her. Don't listen to her. She's crazy!" And then my mother said, "Go outside, and stay outside!" And so then I got outside, and I said, "Well, if I ha—gonna stay out here, then I'm gonna go and I'm not gonna come!" So, then I started running—I was going to go to my friend's house. And then my mother she opened the door and then she said: "What are you—you—you're—you'd better come back, because if you don't, I'm gonna beat the hell of you when you come back!" And so then, I just stopped and I was standin on the corner. And then—and then my—my uncle he came out, cause I think he heard my mother yelling. And then he said, "Anna, what are you doing at this time of the night?" And then he said, "What happened? How come your mother is yelling and everything?" And then I—I started crying, and then he said: "What is it? Is it your mother and your father?" I said, "No," And then I didn't want to talk to him, because I was crying, and I was so nervous. And so then he just walked me home, and he said, "Well, don't cry. I'll go talk to your mother and to your father." And so then he—he walked me home. And then I—I went inside the house, and then my mother said, "Where did you think you were going, stupid?" And I said, "Well, I don't know. I just ran outside the house. I didn't know what—I didn't know whether to go to my friend's house or not." And then—and then my father said, "Go to your room!" And so then I—I went to my room. And then my mother said, "You little ——, one of these days I'm gonna kill you!"

DR: You little—you little what?

TA: You little son-of-a-bitch.

DR: You little son-of-a-bitch—

TA: Mm-hm, and then I started crying, and then I went to my room. And then my uncle he came, and he—he rang the doorbell, and my father said, "Come in!" And so then, my uncle said, "The cops are all out there." And then—but he was just kidding. And then my father said, he started talking to my uncle. And then my mother said—uhhhh. Then my uncle, he told my mother, "What happened? How come you guys are yelling and everything?" And then my mother said, "I dunno—it's this darn kid. And one of these darn days I'm gonna kill her, if she keeps talking back to me!"

DR: Your mother said this to who?

TA: To my uncle.

DR: That's her brother?

TA: Uh-huh. No—uh—

DR: Your dad's brother?

TA: Nomm—cause see his wife is married to—his wife is my mother's—

DR: —sister.

TA: —sister. So then-uh, so then they went to the kitchen and they were talking. And while they were talking I went in and got that bottle of—uh—I donno it's name . . .

DR: Methiolate.

TA: Uh-huh. And then—so then I was standin at the window and I was lookin outside, and I was wondering whether I should drink it or not. So then I said, 'I think I'll call my friend.' And then I called her up and then I said, 'uh-uh'. And the, and then I told her, Maria, I think I'm gonna go to your house, because my mother she's—

DR: —you'd already taken the methiolate?

TA: No, I hadn't taken that yet.

DR: —you hadn't taken it—

TA: So then I told my friend, 'I think I'm gonna drink a bottle of something.' And she said, "No, you'd better not. Huh-uh, you'd *better* not!" And then, and then I said, 'Well, if I don't come over to your house then—I think I'll drink that stuff.' And then she said, "Don't—please don't! OK?" And then I—I just, I just closed that bottle. And then I went back to my room. And I was still crying, because my mother, you know, she was still talking about me—

DR: Um-hm . . .

TA: And—and then—then she started crying, n' and so they—my father he was laughing, but then my—my uncle, he said, "Come on—stop laughing. Look, I'm serious. I- I'm not trying to do this just for—"

DR: What was your uncle doing?

TA: Huh?

DR: What was he saying to you?

TA: No, he was talking to my father.

DR: Oh, you were the one they were talking about—

TA: —uh, huh—

DR: —but your father was laughing at him?

TA: Uh-huh. And—but he was sort of drunk, or something like that, cause he was laughing, you know, he thought that my uncle wasn't serious. So then my uncle said, "God, you shouldn't be fighting in front of the kids. You know, if you fight in front of them, then they get nervous, and then, they don't respect you, because you talk real nasty in front of them and everything. And then—then they would always go around talking about you all, then—then—so then I went back to my room. First I—I went into the bathroom. But then I went to my room. And so then my sister, she went inside—inside my room, and then I told her, 'Get out of here!' And then she said, "No, no! I wanna stay here!" And then I said, 'NO!—if you don't get out, I'm gonna throw you out!' So then she just went out. And then— then she—then I went and got the bottle, and so I had it in my hand—

DR: You had the full bottle?

TA: Uh-huh. And all the time I wonder—and I was wondering whether I should drink it or not. And my sister, she came back inside the room and I told her, "I told you to get out of here." And then, you know, she just stayed looking at me, and she said, "What are you doing with that?" And I said, "Nothing— I'm just—" You know, I didn't give—give her any—any answer. And then, then she said, "You're not gonna drink that, are you?" And then I said, "I don't know." And then my brother, he came inside my room, and then he said, "What're you guys talking about?" And then my sister said, "I don't know. Uh—she wants to take a bath." And then I just got mad and I said, "Get out of here! I told you once!" And then, so they went out and then I just decided to kill myself. —Cause I donno, I was—I was so sick of my mother. You know, you every time—every time that she got mad, she would take it out on me.

These accounts are indicative not only of the extent of the adolescent's alienation from his parents but also serve to point out feelings which resulted from the process discussed earlier in this chapter under "behavioral problems" and "disciplinary techniques," i.e. the adolescent's feeling of abuse stemming from his parents' inappropriate use of discipline and/or rejection.

"ADAPTIVE" VS. "MALADAPTIVE" BEHAVIOR

The last way in which "behavioral problems" are viewed by the author are as "adaptive" vs. "maladaptive" techniques of coping. In order to be able to assess with any accuracy whether or not a set of behaviors is "adaptive" or "mal-adaptive," it would seem advisable to consider at least two important questions, i.e. what was the order in which the behaviors occurred and what were the individuals required to adapt to? For example, it would appear maladaptive in terms of survival to attempt suicide before trying some less drastic form of behavior that was still available and that held some promise of help. Did the suicide attempters attempt suicide "impulsively" before having tried some less drastic means of resolving their problems? An analysis of "behavioral problems" and their sequential ordering, viewed as adaptive techniques, revealed the following. *Thirty out of fifty suicide attempters had gone through all of the categories of adaptive techniques, i.e. 1) rebelling, 2) withdrawing, 3) running away from home, and 4) attempting suicide. In twenty-seven of these thirty cases, the adolescents had attempted to utilize the first three of the less drastic forms of adaptive behavior before having made their first suicide attempt. In short, nearly three fifths of all the suicide attempters using all four categories of adaptation enlisted them in the order of least to most drastic.*

Thirteen out of thirty-one control adolescents utilized exclusively the behaviors associated with the rebellion category. Only four of the thirty-one suicide attempters used this form of behavior exclusively. This points to the fact that for some reason (to be discussed later), many of the control adolescents were able to resolve their problems by using exclusively techniques labeled by psychiatry as "adaptive" (i.e. adolescent rebellion) whereas very few of the suicide attempters succeeded in this.

For the other two possibilities of using one category only, i.e. category two ("withdrawal into self"), or category three, ("running away from home") we find only two cases of suicide attempters and three cases of control adolescents using category two exclusively; and only one suicide attempter and zero control adolescents using category three exclusively. I believe that *this constitutes an important finding, in that it indicates the general reluctance of the suicide attempters and control adolescents to resort initially or exclusively to more drastic forms of adaptation before first having tried less drastic ones.* Only *one* suicide attempter seems to have used the "maladaptive" technique of attempting suicide before having resorted to any of the behaviors associated with categories one, two, or three. In fact, this adolescent seems to have had no prior history of "behavioral problems." His case was also unique in that adaptive forms one, two, or three would have been of no use in helping to resolve his problems since his problems stemmed from poor health. He had in his past experienced a series of operations and was at the time of his attempt about to undergo another. Granting that his health problems led to his progressive isolation from meaningful social relationships, this could not have been resolved by his using adaptive forms one, two, or three in his interpersonal relationships. An increase in meaningful social relationships could have only been achieved through his return to good health, something over which he had no control. Viewed in this context, his case is perhaps not so atypical as it first seemed. It only serves to further illustrate how both the suicide attempters and control adolescents were alike in their reluctance to turn first and/or exclusively to "mal-adaptive" techniques when some less drastic alternative was available. Therefore, with respect to the "appropriateness" of the behaviors as they related to their sequential ordering, *it seems both the suicide attempters and control adolescents met the first criteria of "adaptive" behavior—i.e. that the measures taken to adapt progressed from the least to the most drastic forms of adaptation.*

This brings us to a consideration of the second aspect of the problem: What set of events had the adolescent to "adapt" to? It might be argued that "running away from home" and attempting suicide were mal-adaptive since only one control adolescent tried the former and none resorted to the latter, or that behaviors associated with the "rebellion" category were "adaptive" since more of the control adolescents seem to have used them exclusively. However, this assumes that both the experimental and control adolescents had to contend with similar or at least comparable sets of events in their lives. This would not have been an unreasonable assumption to make at the outset, since the adolescents of the matched pairs ought to have had comparable "life chances." We have already seen that they did not. The suicide attempters had to contend with many more serious, disruptive, unwanted and unanticipated events than the control adolescents. What's more, this situation tended to escalate for the suicide attempters while it stabilized or reduced itself for the adolescents of the control group. Therefore, it seems unwarranted to assume that the control adolescents who adopted only behaviors of "rebellion," and infrequently those of "withdrawal," in order to contend with their problems, had used "adaptive behaviors," while the suicide attempters who had to resort to "rebellion," "withdrawal into self," "running away from home," and suicide attempts had resorted to "mal-adaptive" behaviors. To assume the above is to assume an unfair bias, since *the majority of suicide attempters utilized the same sequence of behavior patterns as the control adolescents, i.e. least to most drastic.* Having tried unsuccessfully to use the techniques used by "normal" adolescents to solve their problems, the suicide attempters finally resorted to whatever techniques remained. The reason that the controls were more successful in resolving their problems with lesser measures need not be seen as the result of different personalities or potentialities, but rather, may well prove to be a function of the fact that they had fewer and less serious problems to deal with. (For a composite picture of the distribution of selected events in the life histories of the thirty-one matched pair adolescents, see Table I in the Appendix.)

From this perspective, the only "maladaptive" course of action for the suicide attempters would have been to stop trying to resolve their problems by whatever available means offered any hope of success. This is the one thing they did not do. There is, of course, another form of adaptation. One might, by whatever means, seek to deny one's reality and by so doing be rid of his problems. If one takes an "abnormal" denial of reality to be a form of adaptation (insofar as it allowed for the survival of the organism), it is one form of "adaptive" behavior conspicuously absent in the experimental adolescents of this sample. Including the forty-eight suicide attempters in the pre-test series, a total of ninety-eight suicide attempters were interviewed. Only one suicide attempter, who was not a part of the study sample, seemed to exhibit such a denial of reality. In general, one was impressed by the attempters' "adult" and accurate assessment of their predicament. If anything, they were too much "with it."

In brief, I feel the indiscriminate use of the term "maladaptive" behavior in reference to adolescent suicide and suicide attempts is unwarranted. It is, I believe, a result of the fact that little attention is paid to the nature or ordering of events in the lives of persons whose behaviors are too often labeled "maladaptive." The term should be used more cautiously until greater study of the two aspects discussed above have been undertaken. There is too great a readiness on the part of those using the "maladaptive" label to assume some form of psychopathology as an explanation of the term, when in fact the symptom, for which the disease is conveniently assumed, may never have existed.

"BROKEN HOMES"

At this point I should like to discuss another concept that those using case history data often refer to in their explanations of suicide, i.e. "broken homes." The life histories of 71 per cent of the suicide attempters and 53 per cent of the control adolescents indicated "broken homes." Eighty-four per cent of the suicide attempters of the non-matched pairs also had "broken homes." The literature on the relationship of "broken homes" in early childhood to suicide and suicide attempts in later life is considerable.)

Dorpat *et al.,* in a review of the psychiatric literature, reported that estimates of broken homes among suicide attempters range from 38 per cent to 84 per cent. Significantly, it is noted that, *"All of the groups of attempted suicides studied were highly selected groups and no data for control groups were given."* [Emphasis added.] [3] In comparing the rates of broken homes among 114 completed suicides and 121 suicide attempters in their own sample, Dorpat *et al.,* found that 63 per cent of the suicide attempters and 50 per cent of the suicides had broken homes. Again, no attempt was made to evaluate the sequential ordering of events: "Where several types of loss occurred for a single subject, categorization was based on the type of loss which occurred first." [4]

My own data indicates that *the thirty-one control adolescents in the author's series had a higher rate of broken homes than the lowest estimate for suicide attempters given by Dorpat. Then, too, why did 71 per cent of thirty-one "matched" suicide attempters with broken homes attempt suicide when 53 per cent of the control adolescents with broken homes did not?*

The answer to this question will not be found in the "significant correlation" of some unidimensional explanation. [Early "childhood traumas" or later "precipitating causes" ought not to be viewed ahistorically. An analysis of "broken homes" which places this event into the context of the adolescent's total biography proved helpful in providing an answer to the above question.)From this perspective, the above rate dilemma proved more apparent than real. For example, although 71 per cent of the suicide attempters and 53 per cent of the control adolescents had experienced broken homes (most of which occurred at an early age), 40 per cent of the suicide attempters' parents had remarried while only 25 per cent of the parents of the control adolescents had done so. Furthermore, the parents of the control adolescents who remarried did so soon after the initial separation, and remained married. The parents of suicide attempters either remarried later in the adolescent's life or, if they remarried early, were subsequently divorced and remarried several more times. The result of this chronology of events is that 58 per cent of the suicide attempters' parents (of the matched pairs) and only 10 per cent of the control adolescents' parents were divorced, separated, and/or remarried since 1959 (or during the escalation stage). Sixty-three per cent of the parents in the non-matched sample of suicide attempters had experienced one or more of the above events during this period. The effects of this sequential ordering of events upon the adolescents should be clear. Whereas both the suicide attempters and the control group adolescents had experienced a high rate of broken homes in early childhood, the control group had experienced a stable home life since the onset of adolescence that the suicide attempters had not. This was especially telling, not only because divorce, separation, death of a parent, or acquisition of a stepparent is a stressful and disruptive event *per se,* but also because it occurred in conjunction with the onset of so many other serious problems for the suicide attempters.

Dorpat *et al.,* contend that their findings lend support to the theories of Bowlby and Zilboorg ". . . that parental loss in childhood predisposes to depression and suicide later in life.[5] My own findings do not support this contention. *Both the suicide attempters and control adolescents had high rates of parental loss in early childhood. One group attempted suicide; the other did not.*

What of the second factor, the relationship between childhood parental loss and depression in later life? This, too, is not supported by the author's findings. *Whereas both the experimental and control groups of adolescents experienced high rates of parental loss in childhood, nearly twice as many suicide attempters of the matched pairs experienced the onset of symptoms of depression ("gloominess," "won't talk," "withdrawal") later in life, i.e., within the last five years. Eighty per cent of the suicide attempters, and only 45 per cent of the control adolescents, experienced one or more of the above symptoms of depression during the escalation stage.*

It is not parental loss in early childhood per se that predisposes to depression and suicide in later life. The loss of a love object is an important aspect of the process, but it must be viewed as part of a process, with particular attention paid to when it occurred and/or reoccurred, and not only to its presence or absence. Furthermore, it seems that it is not the loss of a love object *per se* that is so distressing but the loss of love, i.e. the reciprocal intimacy, spontaneity, and closeness that one experiences in a "primary relationship."

Another aspect to be considered in this regard is whether or not the "object" need be physically absent to be lost. Might not the adolescent experience "loss of a love object" even when one or both of the natural parents are present? I believe that he can. It is clear from the interviews that the suicide attempters were alienated from their parents more frequently, and to a greater degree, than the control adolescents, especially during the second stage.

The relationship of "broken homes" to suicide and suicide attempts has been an issue of central concern in the psychiatric literature. The significance of these concepts is better understood by viewing them as part of a continuing process rather than as some unique traumatic event of early childhood which in and of itself predisposed the individual to depression and suicide in later life. The latter position does nothing to explain why the control adolescents who also experienced a parental loss in early childhood were not disposed to suicide in later life and were far less disposed to symptoms of depression. The author believes that the formulation he has offered above is much more consistent with the data than the traditional psychiatric explanations of how broken homes in early childhood *may* contribute in later life to suicidal tendencies and/or depression.

CONSTRUCTING THE BRIDGE BETWEEN CONSIDERED AND ATTEMPTED SUICIDE

This brings me to the fifth and final stage in the process leading up to an act of suicide. Thus far, I have considered in some detail the social-structural events in the lives of adolescent suicide attempters and a control group of adolescents and the process whereby the ordering of these events led the former to a position of entertaining a "suicide attempt" as a course of action. I have dealt exclusively with the "external" features of the process, in an attempt to find the answers to some of the questions I had originally formulated. What non-shareable problems do suicides or suicide attempters have? How could these be secretly resolved by an act of trust violation (suicide) where the person violates the sacred trust of life? Not only have I previously discussed the nature and ordering of these problems, but I have also reviewed the way in which the suicide attempters (with the progressive failure of "adaptive" techniques) were led to entertain suicide as a possible resolution to their problems. However, there is a qualitative difference between considering suicide, and attempting suicide. The way in which this gap is bridged necessitates a discussion of some "internal" process.

The basis for the formulation of this internal process rests primarily upon an analysis of 112 suicide notes of persons (adults and adolescents) successful in suicide in the Los Angeles area. Suicide notes are used as a source of data because it is presumed by this and other authors that they represent the thoughts and feelings of the suicide at the time of his act.[6] There also seems to be no difference between persons leaving notes and those who do not.[7] The objection may be raised that persons who kill themselves are different from those who only attempt suicide, or that the processes to which adolescent and adult suicides were subject were different from one another. These objections will be dealt with as follows. First, I will present the formulation, and a discussion of it, with respect to the largest category of notes found among the 112 successful suicides. Then I will present, for purposes of comparison, notes by adolescent suicide attempters and those of adolescents successful in suicide. These in turn will be contrasted with the notes of successful adult suicides. Unfortunately, the notes of adults attempting suicide are not available. As Schneidman has indicated, they are exceedingly rare, since the surviving adult usually destroys the note in order not to bring his suicide attempt to the attention of others.[8] The reader will be shown the ways in which all of these categories of persons seemed to be subject to the same process. The suicide notes, the more complete case histories of suicides previously noted in Chapter I, and a comparison of the life histories of the experimental and control adolescents in the author's series, all tend to lend support to the following formulation.

In order to overcome the moral and social constraints against suicide and appear a trust violator, the private individual must 1) be faced with an unexpected, intolerable and unsolvable problem; 2) view this not as an isolated unpleasant incident, but within the context of a long biography of such troubled situations, and the expectation of future ones; 3) believe that death is the only absolute answer to this apparent absolute dilemma of life; 4) come to this point of view by way of, (a) an increasing social isolation whereby he is unable to share his problem with the person or persons who must share it if it is to be resolved, or (b) being isolated from the cure of some incurable disease which in turn isolates him from health and the community, thereby doubly insuring the insolubility of the problem; 5) overcome the social constraints, i.e. the social norms he has internalized whereby he views suicide as irrational and/or immoral, and 6) succeed in this because—as Durkheim pointed out—he feels himself less an integral part of the society than the others and therefore is held less firmly by its bonds, i.e. is less constrained, and 7) accomplish step 6 by applying to his intended conduct—suicide—a verbalization which enables him to adjust his conceptions of himself as a trusted person to his conceptions of himself as a trust violator, and 8) succeed in doing this by defining the situation in such a way that the problem is (a) not of his own making, (b) unresolved not from any lack of effort on his part to deal with it and (c) not given to any resolution known to him excepting death (he doesn't want it this way, but . . . it's "the only way out"); 9) in short, define death as necessary by the above process and in so doing remove all choice and with it sin and immorality, and 10) make some provision for insuring against the reoccurrence of these problems in the afterlife.[9]

The suicide's attempts to deal with life's problems are apparent in the notes. The problem in the final stage is viewed by the potential suicide as not of his own making; he has done all he could to resolve it, but it was not given to any resolution known to him. The problem is not of the moment but is viewed in the context of a long-standing history of problems which have recently escalated to a point that is viewed as insurmountable and exceeding human endurance, so that one cannot simply wait for the "crisis" to pass. The problem *must* be resolved, since it is felt that one cannot live with it. Apart from any private concern with the problem, suicidal persons feel a moral obligation to the public to resolve it, for if they fail, they have become trust violators. The only resolution is seen in death, i.e., it is "the *only* way out." Implicit or explicit in most of the suicide notes is the notion that "they didn't want it this way . . . but . . ." From this perspective, they are now in a position to view themselves as blameless, i.e. trusted persons, while at the same time knowing that you will view them as trust violators because you have not experienced what they have and therefore cannot see the moral and reasonable nature of the act. With this in mind, they beg your indulgence and ask your forgiveness, for, in short, they know what they're doing but they also know you cannot know.

"First Form Notes"

Thirty-five of the 112 suicide notes in this series were "first form notes." Depending upon their length, they expressed all or most of the ten steps described above. These ten steps are incorporated into a six point analysis which accompanies each of the "first form" notes discussed on the following pages. All are characterized by the author's begging forgiveness or requesting the survivors' indulgence. The following examples will serve to illustrate the general tenor.

> To my family and friends:
> I'm sorry it has to be this way. For some reason, I have set unattainable goals for myself. It hurts to live and life is full of so many disappointments and troubles. What I would really like to say is that I can't face up to problems the way I should. Society is always judging you and telling you what to do. My problem I think is that I have always thought only of Bill [himself]. Everything I have done hasn't satisfied me. Why this is I cannot tell you. It is a very funny feeling that I get inside when I sit down to do something. Maybe like what I write or do won't be accepted by society. Competition is another thing I hate. Maybe I expected too much out of life. Please don't cry or feel badly. I know what I am doing and why I am doing it. I guess I never really found out what love or responsibility was.
>
> > Bill
>
> I might also add that I had had in recent years no great desire to continue living. Saying goodbye to all of you who I was close to would only make things harder for me. Believe me I tried to cope with my problems but I couldn't.

Let us examine the note carefully to see how many of the above conditions were met.

The first condition is that the potential suicide views the problem in the final stages as *not of his own making.* At first glance, the note seems to say just the opposite: "For some reason I have set unattainable goals for myself," or ". . . I can't face up to problems the way I should," or "My problem I think is that I have always thought only of Bill [himself]." However, a closer look finds the suicide concluding on this note: *"Believe me, I tried to cope with my problems but couldn't."* What were his problems? "I have always thought only of Bill." If he tried to cope with that he clearly tried to think of persons other than himself, or in Durkheim's terms, be less egoistic, i.e. more an integral part of society. But he couldn't. Another problem was: "Society is always judging you and telling you what to do." He tried to cope with that but couldn't. Then too, society seemed to him to be capricious; he didn't know what to expect: "Maybe like what I write or do won't be accepted by society." He tried to cope with that, i.e. anticipate the expectations of society, but couldn't. "Competition is another thing I hate." He tried to cope with that, i.e. end competition, compete or at least want to compete, but couldn't. Then, too, he "never really found out what love . . . was." All of this leads the suicide to state: "Maybe I expected too much out of life," which is to say, maybe life is full of problems which are impossible to anticipate and which, notwithstanding one's best efforts, must go unresolved. In which case, what is one to do if: "It hurts to live and life is full of so many disappointmentt and troubles."? His problem, ". . . so many disappointments and troubles . . .", was not of his making or choice. The author of the note thus succeeds in viewing it ultimately as something subject to extenuating circumstances and beyond his control.

The second condition is that the suicidal person must feel that *he did all he could to resolve his problems.* Bill, a 17 year-old boy, and the author of this note, tells us: "Believe me I tried to cope with my problems but I couldn't."

Thirdly, the problem must appear to be not of the moment but in the context of a *long-standing history of problems* which escalated of late to a point exceeding human endurance so that one cannot simply wait for it to pass. *"It hurts to live and life is full of so many disappointments and troubles,"* or *"Everything I have done hasn't satisfied me,"* and, further on in the note, "I might also add that I had had *in recent years no great desire to continue living."* [10]

The fourth condition in the author's formulation is that *death must be viewed as necessary,* i.e. "the only way out." The suicide tells us in the first line, "I'm sorry *it has to be this way,"* or again, almost as a reminder in the last line, "Believe me *I tried to cope with my problems but I couldn't."*

Fifth, he is sorry and *begs your indulgence.* "I'm *sorry* it has to be this way." And lastly, *he knows what he is doing; but he also knows you cannot know.* "Please don't cry or feel badly. *I know what I'm doing and why I'm doing it.*"

Keeping these features in mind, let us consider another note of this class.

The following is the suicide note of a teenage switchboard operator and typist.

Dear folks:

I know this won't seem the right thing to you but from where I stand it seems like the best solution, considering what is inevitably in store for the future.

You know I am in debt. Probably not deeply compared to a lot of people but at least they have certain abilities, a skill or trade, or talents with which to make a financial recovery. Yes, I am still working but only "by the grace of the gods." You know how I feel about working where there are a lot of girls I never could stand their cattiness and I couldn't hope to be lucky enough again to find work where I had my own office and still have someone to rely on like Harriet. And above all, most jobs don't pay as well as this one for comparable little work. I get so tired, at typing for instance, that I couldn't hold a straight typist position. I wish I had the social position and "know how" to keep this job. That way I wouldn't worry myself into such a dither that I make stupid errors. Sometimes they're just from trying too hard to turn out a perfect copy or to please someone. With three separate offices served by one board it's pretty hard to locate people for their calls. And when I do find them they don't want to take them— for which I can't blame them as some of them are asinine. But when the calls come in on the board I have to dispatch them one way or another and the fellows don't seem to realize that.

Some girls can talk about their work to their girlfriends and make it sound humorous but I guess it sounds like complaining the way I talk. And when I mention anything to Harriet, either in fun or in an effort to correct a situation, it gets all over the office like wildfire. Now, when I sit there paying attention to the board or my work the fellows think I'm purposely being unfriendly. But just what is there to talk about when you get tired of the same old questions and comments on the weather, "how are you?", "working hard or hardly working?", and you know better than to say very much about things they're interested in or concerned about. I've usually tried to either kid the person concerned about whatever it is or just shut up about it because if one goes about telling the other person's business that can cause trouble. However, the kidding, or even a friendly interest, sometimes, can hurt. So where are you? Might just as well say very little and appear uncooperative or whatever they think.

Due to these and many, many more frustrations from the board and other causes I have become much more nervous than I was. You know what the medicine I was taking did to me so far as my being extremely keyed up, irritable, etc. was concerned. Now I feel just about as depressed as I was keyed up then. I couldn't even talk coherently at times, and now I'm too concerned about my financial affairs to know what it is safe to say. How I wish I could make "small talk" or "party chatter" like some girls do. But I can't compete with most of them for many reasons and after trying to enter into social activities with kids in my age range, especially the past year, I find that I can't compete with most of them. Even if I had all the clothes to look the part I still wouldn't be able to act the part. Sorry I'm such a disappointment to you folks.

I'm saying these things so you'll understand why it's so futile for me to even hope for a better job. And as long as I go on living there will be "working conditions" when there are so many other better places for the money. I don't mean to sound unappreciative of all you folks have done all through the years to keep us kids well and healthy. It's just that I can't see the sense in putting money into a losing game.

The first condition requires that the suicide see their *problems as not of their own making*. What are her problems? The note stipulates the following; she is without money, is currently in debt, is an unskilled worker with a boring job and without prospects for improving her position, about to be fired and without the "know how" to socialize successfully with others or compete with peers. Who was responsible for this situation? First consider her deprived economic status. "I don't mean to sound unappreciative of all you folks have done through the years to keep us kids well and healthy." However, health was all they gave. They could not provide her with either the proper clothing or social graces she needed to get along in the world. "How I wish I could make 'small talk' or 'party chatter' like some girls do. But I can't compete with most of them for many reasons and after trying to enter into social activities with kids in my age range, especially in the past year, I find that I can't compete with most of them. *Even if I had all the clothes to look the part, I still wouldn't be able to act the part."*

Who was responsible for the fact that she was about to be fired? The suicide tells us that she might not be fired if she had her own office as she used to. This would help her to reduce her irritability, a condition resulting from her inability to successfully interact with others. Unfortunately, ". . . I couldn't hope to be lucky enough again to find work where I had my own office . . ." The dilemma is that even if she could hope for it, being isolated in her own office, while it would avoid potential conflict situations, would also isolate her from any prospects of establishing a meaningful social relationship, i.e., she would not ". . . still have someone to rely on like Harriet."

As for managing to do what is necessary to retain even her current unsatisfactory situation, she sees her prospects as nil. "With three separate offices served by one board, it's pretty hard to locate people for their calls. And when you do find them, they don't want them . . . But when the calls come in on the board I have to dispatch them one way or another and the fellows don't seem to realize that." What other reasons are there for her job being in jeopardy? These are described in some detail in the third paragraph of the note. The gist of this is that her intentions and efforts to be sociable are continually being misunderstood by others. In self defense, and in order to avoid the conflicts stemming from these misunderstandings, she stops talking to her co-workers and appears uncooperative. In sheer desperation, she abdicates and lets the others think what they will. In summing up, she tried her best to overcome the problem of not being able to "fit in", but failed. If people were not constantly misunderstanding her, and realized she *had* to dispatch calls, that she was *trying* to be sociable, etc., she would not have reached the state of resignation and desperation that she felt at the time of the note-writing. It is clear from the note that she certainly did not want it this way. The tenor of the note is "if they had only . . .", she would not have felt, and consequently acted as she did. In a further effort to deal with these problems, she took some medicine so as to feel less irritable, and better be able to cope with her predicament. What happened? Rather than reduce her irritability it made her depressed and even less able to deal effectively with her problems. The sum total of the above experiences resulted in her feeling that she was not responsible for her problems and that she had certainly done everything possible to resolve them.

What of the second step, a *longstanding history of problems?* Most of the problems cited at the start of step one were of long standing; being in debt, her economic deprivation, lacking in skills, trade or talent with which to make a financial recovery, low job satisfaction, no prospects for improvement, and her inability to successfully interact or compete with peers, were some of her more obvious longstanding problems.

Third, the *escalation of problems* beyond human endurance: "How I wish I could make 'small talk' or 'party chatter' like some girls do. But I can't compete with most of them for many reasons, and after trying to enter into social activities with kids in my age range, *especially in the last year,* I find that I can't compete with most of them," or "Due to these and many, many more frustrations from the board and other causes *I have become much more nervous than I was.*"

Fourth step: death is seen as inevitable. "I am saying these things so you'll understand *why it's so futile for me to even hope* for a better job." Or, "it's just that I can't see the sense in putting money into a *losing game.*" Or, "I know this won't seem the right thing to you, but from where I stand it seems like the best solution, *considering what is inevitably in store for the future.*"

Fifth: *beg your indulgence:* "Sorry I'm such a disappointment to you folks." Or, *"I don't mean to sound unappreciative* of all you folks have done all through the years to keep us kids well and healthy."

Sixth, *"I know what I'm doing but I know you cannot know.":* "I know this won't seem the right thing to you, but from where I stand it seems like the best solution . . ."

The following is a third note by an 18 year-old student who committed suicide at a college in the Los Angeles area. It is one that incorporates all of the features of the other notes, as well as provision for a better life in the hereafter.

> Dad.
>   Im am (sorry) I tried everything but nothing seemed to help. I was afryed to live because I was alone. I asked Margaret for help but I didn't get any. I beegged and prayed with all my heart but she couldn't come back when I needed her most. I love her dad and I love you and Mom. I am sorry I couldn't find help but thats the way it gose. Sorry your son, Gary. P.S. "over"
>   To Margaret. I love you and I no it now. Im sorry it was to late. There is nothing I could say that would make you see what was happening to me. I am sorry.
>   Evens in heavens. Ill love Margaret and Ill wate for you there.
>   Gary.

The suicide feels his problems are about to cease. After all, all's well in heaven and he's going there to wait.

All three of the above notes were written by adolescent suicides: the first and third by teen-age boys, the second by a teen-age girl. Let us now compare these "first form" notes (the most popular among adolescent and adult suicides) with a note from an adolescent suicide attempter. The following is a letter from a 17 year-old Negro male to his father. The letter was written the day before the adolescent's suicide attempt (his second) took place.

Dear father

I am addressing you these few line to let you know that I am fine and everyone else is and hope that you are the same. Daddy I understand I let you down and I let mother down in the same way when I did that lil ole thing that wednesday night. daddy I am sorry if I really upset you, but daddy after I got back I realized how sad and bad you felt when I came back to California, but daddy I am not happy out here and I not happy down there. I just didn't know what to do. I had lost my best girl a week before I did that. I had a fight because so dude tried to take advantage of her when I split to the store so I came back I heard a lot of noise like bumping so I goes on in and there hee is trying to rape my girl and my best one to. So we had a little hassel and he came back with some of his friends you know to get me. So I called up some of my friends and they got to fighting and pretty soon it just turned into a slauter and so a few days later I lost my girl. Her best girl friend wanted me but I didn't want her so she told Barbara a whole bunch of lys and so the broad wanted to believe her so we had a little argument. So I just desided that I would put all of my troubles in one big boat and let it sink but I was found just before I died and another thing Daddy that bothered me a lot was Mary Lou. And I knew just how much I love her and I knew just how much you love me and how it hurted to see me go but daddy I felt the same thing all the way out here and I still think the same thing. daddy you don't know just how much I really wanted to stay with you but something somewhere kept telling me to go back to your mother. Then I would say I know my father and mother both love me so I just hate to breake people hearts so I said to myself I hope my daddy please understand I still loved him even though I was going to come back home. but, daddy even though mother reased of you kids there is no reason for me to say I don't want to stay with you but daddy I understand what it means to you to have had me stay with you daddy. Now sence I came out the and stayed longer than I should have because after I found out I didn't like it and the name of the town itself I decided I would stay as long as I could before school started or just before Christmas came. So daddy please come out for Christmas and see if you like it or do like Lou Ann did got a pass and came out here and she didn't like it so she say and she went back to Mt. Clemens. Oh yes daddy Mother said answer her letter, and dad forgive me for the thing that I did but daddy just don't know just how much I bare. I am not trying to say that mother is not trying to help me but daddy that little old woman can't take to much more of this so daddy would you please come out this year and try to help us get back on our feet again and I am talking about all of us when I came home an and did the wrong thing look like the world stoped with me. So daddy i am back at home now I been here for about a week now and I have started to school.

But daddy I still haven't gotten everything I need so daddy could you please send me some money this week. Well dad tell everyone hello and give my regards to all and tell Ruby and Miss Smith I haven't forgotten them and I will write.

But the reason I hadn't wrote you when I first got he daddy I had a little something to see about and I was kind of shook up for a while I was accused of having been responsible for having 3 girl knock up and they were suppose to all be mine but daddy I proved it wasn't my fault that they were pregnant because I hadn't touch but one and she helped me beat that by saying that it wasn't mine. But it was the boy who she had went out with when I was up in Mt Clemens and daddy if—don't tell Judy or Mother cause if you tell Judy she have it all ove town. and if you tell mother she will get worried everytime I get a phone call or a girl drop by the house and I be talking to the girl so will stay right close so that she can hear what is going on and yet it has to be told I tell it ok. daddy. Oh and she wouldn't let Judy go out any more boy until she get 16 or 17, and that would mean Judy would try to sneak away every little chance she get just like Rays girl she had a baby before I met her and now she is pregnant again and her father did her like that and you see what happened to her don't you. and I don't think I could stand to see Judy like that she is too for sex and things of that nature so daddy please don't write back here or anyplace and say so someone will get the word to mother. Daddy I don't want you to think that is the only reason I came up tho and the only reason I wouldn't stay is because I wanted to come back and start that same old dope drag over. Well, that is not it but because I find more people out here and I am talking about girls only. daddy the kind of person I am and the thing I used to do I don't want Judy or William or anyone else in the family to follow that or part of the path that I blaze you see daddy just before I came out here I tried to be a pimp and when I came back here I tried once more and I had fail but not bad because I live on my name alone. mostly every one on the west side of L.A. knew the name of Jones, but daddy when I was there you seem so happy until I just couldn't ruin the only joy you had, so I sad as I sat and thought it over up there because you had a good name and I said I don't want my father to just what kind of a son he had. So I decided to come home before I get in some kind of trouble up here and take or ruin my home up here but daddy I just couldn't get used to your city. I not saying just because it is small or anything but it was just some of the people up there. I mean out in M.C. if you are a stranger and don't know any better you try to talk to any mans woman that you don't know and man might just know you from out of town and trying to pull his woman then he ready to kill you for nothing but out here there are women everywhere you look and most of them are not married so you don't have to worry about getting jumped on like I did not at school I seen so pretty nice women and I would talk to a few but you see up there is you look as good as I do and you from a big city well naturally a girl if he really dig you then you ask her to let you talk to her and do she have an old man she will say no she don't. and out here you just about believe these here women they are alright, and we have enough women in L.A. to give every man in Mt. Clemens 3 or 4 thousand wives and you can just about depend on them. You remember when the boys tried off me that time. I knew I would have had to kill a few of them or someone else. Because well I am not trying to brag or anything of that nature but I was thing that could every happen to Mt. Clemens but there was only one stop and that one was the women. and another thing I didn't like the part where you have to walk and see the women let them come to you if they need you that bad. Daddy this is true, out here I never have picked up a telephone receiver and dialed and asked for a girl but daddy every one don't do women like I do. and daddy, if all of the little women were coming to school then you know there wouldn't be anymore me. Now if you think that I am trying give you than ask anyone or as many as you like that I have just put my arms around they will tell what I will do for them and daddy ask wasn't I choice about who or how I kissed and no one girl that flip her lid the first time I kissed her and at first you know the first night I met her. The second night I to her to the show and when you came up ther and picked us up did you notice that she was kinda mad but when she invited me into her house she really went wild when I told her that I couldn't kiss or make love to her or ask her to go with be because I tried to explain it to her that I wouldn't be very long before I go back to L.A. and so she said I want you for the time you are and so I look at her but you had told me her heart belong to another so I told her she was the fool and she said so I still want you. and then she aske you don't like me do you don't want to kiss me either and so I soft spot in my heart. And so I kissed her and from then until now she will tell you just what she said and did that night and everytime I would see her and I almost got into a fight about her me and this boy. Of you know Sam's brother almost had to get it on. At least they could act civilized and ask you are you are you any real on between but instead they rather stick you in the back with a knife. I ran out of ink so I use this pencil. and daddy out here if a boy and girl fight well they throw the boy in jail, and if you are fighting with another man and she not your wife you sit in for about 16 hours and they let you go if that is you first time but if you been there twice for the same thing then they can charge you with anything she say you did to her boyfriend the one she had locked up and a wholie bunch of boy don't jump on one girl and try to rape her. and the so called parties they have daddy they are so different because when you go to a party to have a good time up there the people just sit around and don't dance. the first time I appear on the sene of a party people are getting ready to kill me because I me (make) them all look sick and the first party I went didn't noone dance but me I kept asking the girls to dance with me and so I was dancing by myself and all the females wanted to try to buy me but I knew to me if the would think sociable then it wouldn't be so bad. and those guys won't stick together now right after I got jumped on I arganized a lil gang called the Nortons and that the name of a gang around here where I live so after planing for about I figured out a way to catch of the boys across town that thought they were bad we had every kind of something that could kill a man then the minute came when we were going to attack and somebody name Smith said let wait until tomorrow so I could keep that together so one more thing the people out there get ugly minds and they nosey. Well one way . . . PS daddy do you really think Mt. Clemens has more to offer than L.A.? L.A. IS WHERE I STAY BY FOR NOW ANSWER SOON

LOVE WILLIAM

Daddy I tried as hard as I could to make it cheerful but it dose get sad.

(turn over)

Daddy I am up by myself I been up all night trying to write you something to cheer you up because I could your heart breaking when you first asked Stan's wife if they would have room and that Sunday dad it hard but I fought the tears that burned my eyes as we drove off and daddy part of my sickness when I had taken an overdose I did just want to sleep myself away because I missed you dad you made me feel like I just found where I belong just like a lost piece of puzzle.

But when I left I felt like I had killed something inside of an I knew you hated to see me go and I hated to go to but daddy well I knd of missed mother and after I had see her I miss you and I remembered what you said I settle down but daddy I tried hard so I went and bought some sleeping pill and took so both of you could feel the same thing.

How many of the six conditions found in the notes of the adolescent suicides' discussed above are found in this suicide attempter's note? Consider the first of these, i.e. *the problem is not of his own making*. What was the problem? As the letter states, and my formulation provides, there were many problems; the separation of his parents, poverty, the loss of his best girl, being accused of fathering three children by three different girls, and taking dope (which the case history revealed alienated his mother). However, the leitmotif of the letter is his progressive isolation from meaningful social relationships in general and the problem of being torn between the love of his separated parents in particular. ". . . and that Sunday dad it hard but I fought the tears that burned my eyes as we drove off and daddy part of my sickness when I had taken an overdose I did just want to sleep myself away because I missed you dad you made me feel like I just found where I belong just like a lost piece of puzzle. But when I left I felt like I had killed something inside of an I knew you hated to see me go and I hated to go to but daddy well I kind of missed mother and after I had see her I miss you and I remembered what you said I settle down but daddy I tried hard so I went and bought some sleeping pill and took so both of you could feel the same thing."

He was not responsible for his parents separating nor, in spite of his every effort, was he able to find a way of uniting them. The last line of this note is characteristic of a phenomenon I have sometimes encountered in my interviews with suicidal adolescents. I refer to it as an "equality principle." It takes the form of "if they don't care . . . I don't either," or "I bought some sleeping pills and took (them) so both of you could feel the same thing," etc. I feel this principle is sometimes invoked by the adolescent in order to accomplish either one or both of the following, i.e. it is an attempt to resolve the status difference between adolescence and adulthood, and/or it is used to resolve some otherwise irresolvable problem as in the case of the note cited above.

The second condition is a *long-standing history of problems.* Evidence of this is found in his long separation from his father, being torn between the love of the mother and father, the poverty status of the family, his dope addiction, and pimping.

Third, the *escalation of problems* of late, beyond endurance, is also stipulated in the note: someone tried to rape his best girl, the loss of his best girl, the "culture shock" of urban to rural shift when he went to see his father, the first suicide attempt, being accused of paternity by three girls, etc. Regarding the above, he tells us in the opening lines of the letter, ". . .dady after I got back I realized how sad and bad you felt when I came back to California, but dady I'm not happy here and I not happy down there. I just don't know what to do." Because of this escalation of problems and the apparent lack of any resolution to them, "I just decided that I would put all of my troubles in one big boat and let it sink . . ."

The fourth condition of the process, *that death must be seen as necessary,* is also provided for. "I'm not happy out here and I not happy down there. I just don't know what to do." Then, too, if he favored one parent, the other suffered. "Dady you don't know just how much I really wanted to stay with you but something somewhere kept telling me to go back to your mother." There was only one impartial way that both "could feel the same thing." Suicide was, in fact, *the only way that he could resolve all of his problems and theirs, simultaneously.*

Next, he *begs their indulgence.* "Daddy I understand I let you down and I let mother down in the same way when I did that lil ole thing [the suicide attempt] that wednesday night." ". . . forgive me for the thing I did (*but I know what I'm doing and I know that you can't know*) but daddy you don't know just how much I bare."

How do the notes of adult suicides conform to the conditions of "first form" notes and compare with the notes of adolescent suicides and suicide attempters? The following is an example. I will leave it up to the reader to analyze it and decide for himself the extent to which it adheres to the six stages previously outlined. The psychiatric view would anticipate that the notes of adult and adolescent suicides and suicide attempters would be very different, not only because they have different sets of personal problems, but also because adolescents are thought to act much more impulsively.

I believe this is not at all the case. All of the notes in the author's series seem to be the same or at least very similar in form.

My Dearest Ones

When you get this it all be over for me on earth but just the beginning of my punishment for what I have done to you all. I am truly sorry, if you can believe that. I have tried to find myself but it seems I lost myself somewhere, I have done my best to figure out when it was and what caused it to happen but it seems to me it has been happening all my life. You all have been more than anyone could expect. I love you very much, —I know you will find this hard to believe after what I have done to you and am about to do to myself and you. I believe in my heart you will be better off without me and you can make some kind of life for yourselves better than the one I have given you. Kids try and remember some of the good things about me if you possibly can. I have given what I am about to do lots of thought and each time I have thought about it there seems no other way. Harry, you and Willi try your best to grow up to be honest, honorable men, I suppose the one thing I am leaving you is an example not to follow under any circumstances even for a moment. Helen you are well on your way just keep on in that direction. Jane, you and Joan be nice girls and good women just be like mother and you will be the best. My darling wife, I love you and thank you for those years we had together. If it were possible I would like to try and do it different again. I have been so confused and still am that I can't say all the things I would like to even though this is my last chance. I considered doing this several days ago but decided not to ruin your Christmas but the time has come for me to go so my darling good-bye forever, I don't know what's on the other side perhaps it will be worse than here. If I can I'll look in on your dreams, and pass a thought to you. Mama, Daddy, Rose, Sonny and Shirley good-bye.

Thanks for everything to the Johnsons and theirs.

I love you all May God help me and forgive me for what I am about to do.

Again Good-Bye.

Jack and Daddy

What I have attempted to do through the above analysis was to demonstrate the way in which "first form" suicide notes left by adolescent suicide attempters, adolescent suicides and adult suicides all have in common a formal set of characteristics which are helpful in understanding the perspec-

tive of the actor and how he came to entertain suicide as a rational course of action.

However, not all suicide notes are "first form" notes. Since I do not have a large enough number of notes from suicide attempters at my disposal to compare them with the other forms that suicide notes sometimes take, I will not at this point involve the reader in a detailed analysis of these other forms, an analysis which entails and deserves a more complete treatment than can be provided for here. Instead, I will offer a brief outline of the remaining forms found in the 112 notes in the author's series.

The analysis revealed *four other categories of notes:* "Illness notes" of two sorts (those in which the authors express in some form the idea of being "sorry," and those in which no appeal for indulgence is expressed), notes of "direct accusation," "last will and testaments," and "notes of instruction." In all, there were about thirty-four illness notes. The number of "sorry" and "not-sorry" illness notes were about equal. The number of conditions described in "first form" notes that were also found in illness notes depended primarily upon their length. The two formal distinguishing features of "illness" notes were that they may or may not have begged forgiveness and, secondly, that the source of the problem was generally better defined than in the "first form" notes and restricted to the area of poor health and/or increasing pain and its social and personal implications for the individual. I believe the reason why the authors of "illness notes" may or may not have begged the survivor's forgiveness rested upon the suicide's belief that the public may or may not in the case of illness have made an exception to its usual indignation at suicide. That some, but not all, have made this exception is generally recognized. To quote from one of the "not sorry" illness notes, "Surely there must be a justifiable mercy death." If there was a justifiable death by suicide, one would not have to apologize for it. It was, I believe, the ambiguity surrounding this question that was responsible for about one-half of the notes requesting forgiveness, and the other half omitting such requests.

A second form of notes omitting requests for indulgence on the part of the survivors was the "direct accusation" note. This, too, seems understandable since the writer held that not only was the problem not of his own making, but he knew who was responsible for his having to commit suicide. In such cases, the author was righteously indignant and omitted requests for indulgence, especially when the note was directed at the guilty party. Ten of the 112 notes took this form. These notes were usually very brief, sometimes only a line long.

The third and fourth categories of notes—"last will and testaments" and "notes of instruction"—also excluded requests for forgiveness. These were usually brief and to the point. None admitted guilt, nor did they usually discuss the circumstances surrounding the suicide. There were nine notes of "will and testament" and fourteen notes of "instructions."

Only ten notes were atypical and fell into a "residual category." One distinguishing feature was that four of these had the only element of humor found in all the notes. Having affixed a garden hose to the exhaust of his car in order to asphyxiate himself, one victim attached this note to the dashboard of his car: "Do not disturb; someone sleeping."

FOOTNOTES

1. Alfred Schutz, *Collected Papers, Vol. I. The Problem of Social Reality* (The Hague: Martinus Nijhoff, 1962), p. 11.

2. The following discussion is based upon an article by the author entitled "Broken Homes and Social Isolation in Attempted Suicides of Adolescents," *International Journal of Social Psychiatry*, Vol. XIII, No. 2, 1967, 139–149 (with Joseph D. Teicher).

3. Theodore L. Dorpat *et al.*, "Broken Homes and Attempted and Completed Suicide," *Archives of General Psychiatry*, XII (February 1965), 213.

4. *Ibid.*, p. 214.

5. *Ibid.*, p. 216.

6. Jacob Tuckman *et al.*, "Emotional Content of Suicide Notes," *The American Journal of Psychiatry*, July 1959, p. 59.

7. *Ibid.*, p. 59.

8. Edwin S. Shneidman and Norman L. Farberow, "Genuine and Simulated Suicide Notes," in *Clues to Suicide*, edited by Edwin S. Shneidman and Norman L. Farberow (New York: McGraw Hill Book Company 1957), 198.

9. Jerry Jacobs, "A Phenomenological Study of Suicide Notes," *Social Problems*, XV, No. 1 (Summer 1967), 60–72. For a fuller description of the tenth step see pages 70 through 72 of this article, or "The Use of Religion in Constructing the Moral Justification of Suicide" by Jerry Jacobs in *Deviance and Respectability: The Social Construction of Moral Meanings*, edited by Jack D. Douglas, Basic Books, 1970. The discussion revolving around the process whereby one succeeds in "Constructing the Bridge Between Considered and Attempted Suicide" was based primarily upon the above article, "A Phenomenological Study of Suicide Notes."

10. The suicide had, in the above regard, much in common with Goethe's romantic hero, Werther. Werther, in discussing with Albert (a friend of his) the recent suicide of a young girl, loses patience with Albert's lack of empathy and says to him:

> Shame on him who can look on calmly and say, "Foolish girl! She should have waited; she should have let time wear off the impression; her despair would have been eased, and she would have found another lover to comfort her." One might as well say, "The fool, to die of a fever! Why did he not wait till his strength was restored, till his blood became calm? All would have gone well, and he would have been alive now."

Johann Wolfgang von Goethe, *The Sorrows of Young Werther* (New York: Rinehart and Co., 1958), p. 51.

CHAPTER 4

Conclusions and Implications
for Suicide Prevention

Chapter 1 dealt with a four-way perspective from which to view the literature on suicide, i.e., the morphological and etiological approaches in conjunction with a conscious-rational or unconscious-irrational model. A discussion of these perspectives revolves ultimately around methodological questions related to a philosophy of science. The issue is not only how many logical inconsistencies are found within this or that "systematic" explanation of suicide, but rather how many of the assumptions made "for the time being," within any particular theory, can be presented in such a way as to be given to empirical testing at some future date. Whether or not a statement is capable of meeting this condition is a key feature in whether or not such statements fall within the realm of scientific inquiry or must remain within the domain of metaphysical speculation.

PROBLEMS WITH EXISTING PERSPECTIVES

I have attempted to show that postulating an unconscious-irrational element as an explanation of suicide can never fulfill the above condition. "Ids," "egos," and "superegos," are concepts created to explain social and personal feelings and behaviors. However, as Mills points out, they cannot themselves be formulated in such a way as to be given to empirical falsification. As such, they are metaphysical propositions, useful at some point in time for inferring answers to questions that otherwise seem without an answer. To the extent that one is successful in reformulating the problem in such a way that an answer to the question can be offered which allows for others to credit or discredit it on empirical grounds, such a formulation of the problem, as it relates to the pursuit of a social "science," must be seen as preferable. It is just such a formulation for the study of suicide that I have attempted to present in this book.

I believe there is good reason for sociology to reevaluate the merit of the methodology it has abandoned since Durkheim's success in *Suicide*. I believe this success was based more upon his eloquence than the strength of his argument. It was Durkheim, ironically, who was a strong supporter of the morphological approach as constituting a proper methodology for the "scientific" study of social phenomena. His reasons for abandoning it, without having first attempted it, seem to the author unfounded. There is, I believe, a common denominator to the life situations of suicides and, in my opinion, their life histories and suicide notes constitute both a legitimate and useful source of data. One way to overcome the criticisms of Durkheim is to use these data in a way that allows for an explanation of suicide in a process rather than in some independent event. Further, we would do well to do as Durkheim did, and define suicide. Having done so, we would do well to do as he did not, and consider for study only those cases that adhered to the definition. I feel as Durkheim did, that such a definition needs to incorporate an aspect of intentionality. How best to arrive at an individual's intentions after the fact presents a difficult question. All existing "lethality scales," it seems to me, are inadequate. The failings of some of these schemes will be discussed toward the end of this chapter. One way to avoid the problem of inferring the intentionality of dead persons might be to see if suicide attempters were subject to the same process as suicides and, if so, try to gain some insight into their intent through interviews reconstructing the events leading up to their feelings at the time of the attempt. *I feel that suicides and suicide attempters have been subject to the formal aspects of the same or a very similar process.* The possibility of establishing intent from this perspective has been discussed in Chapter 3. Letters and notes left by suicides and suicide attempters, to the extent that they are held to contain the feelings and beliefs of the suicide at the time of his act, also provide important clues to intentionality. This was discussed under the section dealing with suicide notes. Finally, the diaries of suicides, a few of which were referred to in Chapter 1, provide an invaluable source of data for the study of suicide and the establishment of intent.

In brief, the use of the above materials within the perspective set forth by the author in this thesis offers promise of finding the "essential characteristics" of suicide. Whether or not it will also prove useful in explaining suicide rates seems to me a less important question, until such time as one has better reason to suppose that official suicide rates are in fact indicative of the number of "suicides." Much remains to be done to establish these "essential characteristics" and, as Durkheim was well aware, many detailed case histories would be required to succeed in such an undertaking. The author does not have many detailed case histories. However, judging from the fifty case histories of suicide attempters that I do have, and the few thorough case histories of suicides collected by others, as well as accounts found in the notes of suicides and the suicide attempters, one can already begin to delineate these characteristics in the formal aspects of a process to which it seems all of the above were subject. I believe such an encouring start should inspire greater effort by sociologists in the use of the case history approach. The almost exclusive use of the etiological approach for over half a century, and its lack of success in offering a consistent answer to the question of social-suicide rates or any answer at all to the question of why any particular person suicides and any other one does not, warrants, I believe, a reevaluation of its use.

Granting that the prediction of suicide for any particular person was not the task that Durkheim set himself, the contradictory findings discussed in Chapter 1, as well as the methodological problems inherent in the use of "official suicide rates" (by those seeking to explain suicide rates, if not suicide, through the etiological approach) leave much to be desired. Those concerned with a predictive index for anticipating suicide in particular persons, i.e., the psychiatrists and psychologists, have also thus far been eminently unsuccessful. Such concepts as unconscious-irrational, impulsive act, frustration-aggression models, insanity, broken homes and loss of love object in early childhood, as well as psychiatric diagnostic categories, all seem without much merit in explaining, anticipating or preventing suicide. Apart from the difference in focus, the number of contradictions found within the medical model are approximated only by those found within the etiological approach. Stengel et al. had this to say:

> This brief survey of the main trends in suicide research will convey an idea of the volume and variety of work in this field. The body of knowledge which has accrued is considerable, but its usefulness for prediction and prevention of suicidal acts has still to be proved, and there is no evidence that it has had any influence on the suicide rates. This is disappointing, considering the efforts spent in this field over almost a century.[1]

AN ALTERNATIVE OUTLOOK

I believe that one way to overcome these inconsistencies and establish a scientific perspective toward the study of suicide is to incorporate what I feel is the best of both systems, i.e. the use of case history materials, suicide notes, diaries, etc., and the abandonment of "clinical insight" as a means of "interpreting" these data. One might instead seek the common denominator to suicide in the suicide's own accounts, first by taking these accounts seriously, and secondly by seeking the causes of suicide in the formal aspects of a process rather than in some independent event.

A further necessity, that of viewing suicide as stemming from a conscious-rational choice, is given by a fact that Durkheim at first insisted upon, and later abandoned, the concept that acts lacking in volition are excluded by definition from being suicides. To speak of unconscious choice seems to me a contradiction in terms. If one is unaware of his reasons for choosing, and does not anticipate the results or reasons for his act, how can it be said that one has chosen at all? What is more, it is hard to imagine how one could substitute another definition that might be more meaningful without allowing that the actor was aware in advance of the consequences of his act and/or that he had some idea of why he selected that act over others. Granting that it is no easy matter to establish intent, the resolution of this problem will not be found in denying it. I have offered earlier some means by which to pursue, within the context of empirical referents, the intent and motives of suicides. To accept the etiological approach of Durkheim as "given" would be to deny the necessity of establishing intent or motives in suicide. To accept a medical model would be to recognize the need for an answer to this question, while denying any "scientific" means of achieving it. The reader is referred to the earlier critique of C. Wright Mills on pages 11–12, and the long list of failures with respect to the prediction and prevention of suicide noted on page 105. After over 100 years of pursuing the assumptions of the medical model the above record should, in the author's opinion, give some pause for reflection.

I believe the methods and models presented in this thesis promise a way out of this dilemma. In doing so, they may also provide a means of anticipating suicide in particular persons. Granting that this would require a thorough case history of the individual, including the circumstances he had encountered, in what order, and how he "experienced" them, such a task is not impossible, especially among certain social groups of "captive audiences." There is, I believe, at present no litmus test for establishing suicide potential. Many have made such claims, but none have been very successful in predicting or preventing suicide. For example, and I quote here from an article entitled "Potential Suicides—What To Look For," *The Journal of the American Medical Association.* Dr. Ross had these tips to offer:

> One's first observation may be of a pale-faced, sallow person sitting huddled in a waiting-room chair, evidencing little or no spontaneous activity. Further inspection reveals an accentuation of the facial wrinkles and eyelid folds, a lack-luster to the hair, some evidence of weight and sleep loss. Carelessness or even unkempt grooming may also be noted. . . . When one shakes hands with the patient, he may become aware of the various stigmata of underlying emotional tone through psychophysiologic communications: warmth, dryness, dampness, cold, clammy, firm, list-

less, forceful, weak, and the like . . . Loss of appetite is apt to be marked and sustained. But in other cases food may be used as a tranquilizer, leading to over-eating and obesity.[2]

I suggest that detecting suicidal persons by the above criteria would entail more luck than insight into the ways of "psychophysiologic communications." Farberow *et al.,* in an article entitled "The Suicidal Patient and the Physician," state in a section devoted to an "Evaluation of Suicidal Potentiality":

> The course of action for the physician in handling cases identified or suspected as suicidal will depend to a large extent on the evaluation of the seriousness of the suicidal potentiality. This is not a particularly difficult task and can be done relatively quickly by the physician . . .[3]

The author believes there is good ground for skepticism regarding these and other statements as they relate to establishing the actor's intent.

POTENTIAL USES OF THE AUTHOR'S FORMULATION FOR THE DETECTION AND PREVENTION OF SUICIDE

The processes described by the author on the preceding pages should be of particular interest to educators and others interested in the prevention of suicide among school age children. While it is true that there is no convenient way of detecting the potential suicide in a school setting through the use of the author's formulation (or any other known to him), the studies' findings indicate that certain steps can be taken to help prevent school children from becoming suicidal. However, the initiation of these preventive measures will require that school personnel reorient their goals, at least in part, to better achieve what the adolescents saw as the school's main virtue, i.e. to provide a place for them to meet and socialize with each other. Remember, the suicide attempt resulted from what the adolescent viewed as a complete breakdown of meaningful social relationships. As a potential source of relief for overcoming this social isolation the school held great promise. First and perhaps foremost was the fact that school attendance was compulsory. This served to bring the isolated adolescent into a situation that was at the very least, a potential source of assistance. If he were not a "captive audience" the withdrawn adolescent might have for a variety of reasons, secluded himself entirely from others, and from the possibility of establishing and perpetuating the meaningful relationships he sought. The compulsory nature of formal education helped to overcome this initial and crucial drawback to any successful suicide prevention measure. However, the problem still remained that while the students saw the school primarily as a place to socialize, their efforts to do so were thwarted by the school's personnel who viewed it, first and foremost, as an institution of learning. If the school personnel had realized the importance of the school to the adolescent in his search for meaningful relationships, and done something to help implement the adolescents' efforts through a system of planned programs, it would have gone a long way towards reducing suicides and suicide attempts among the school aged children of this study. Programs designed to increase and extend interaction between troubled students and their peers and teachers, apart from increasing the potential for establishing meaningful interactions, and reducing the potential for suicide, would serve another purpose as well.

In addition to helping to arrest suicide and suicide attempts, it would help reduce the number of "drop-outs." *About one third of the adolescent suicide attempters seen by the author had dropped out of school recently. Eighty-nine per cent of these adolescents "dropped out" for reasons other than scholarship.* The benefits of a school-based suicide prevention program along the lines suggested above can also be viewed as helping to solve a public health problem. This is true not only because of the potential for suicide prevention, but because many of the adolescents in our sample had symptoms of illness diagnosed as "functional physical complaints not given to specific diagnosis." In short, in many cases, adolescents apparently had nothing physically wrong with them when they saw a doctor. Forty-six per cent of all the adolescent suicide attempters seen reported some contact with doctors for physical or mental complaints within the year of the attempt. All were seen by doctors at the time of the attempt.

In the light of this and other findings, the author believes that in many cases, the suicidal adolescent consulted a physician, not for the relief or cure of a particular symptom, but rather for the potential source of help implicit in the physician's role. The analogy of the doctor functioning as a "secular priest" is a common one. Not only is the doctor's position unique in terms of providing the suicide attempter with access to what he may feel is a potential source of help when all others have failed, but the doctor as well as the priest is one of the few persons to whom one feels free to confide and/or confess. This is a function of the objectivity, impartiality, confidentiality, and anonymity the seeker assumes of the doctor-patient or priest-parishioner relationship. No less important to those seeking help is the presumption that the doctor and priest hold "offices" in the two most powerful existing agencies of help: science and religion.

With this in mind it is clear that while the application of the author's formulation for the detection of suicidal persons in school settings is impractical on a large scale, its potential in a doctor-patient interactional context is considerable. Not only may the doctor (as the teacher and peer) serve to help prevent or a least postpone a suicide attempt by acting (even temporarily) as a "significant other," but the doctor because of his status and role is in a position to search by the methods outlined above, for those processes that lead to suicide and suicide attempts. Should these evidence themselves in the course of the physician taking the patient's history, he could then intervene on the patient's behalf. While the potential exists for the doctor to act as an important agent in the prevention of suicide, only the potential is there. Whether or not this potential is realized, depends upon the doctor expending the additional time and effort necessary to accomplish, first, the recognition of the potential suicide, and secondly, some means of directly or indirectly coming to his aid through a course of action that will have to rely primarily upon milieu manipulation. As things currently stand the prospects are not bright. The thing furthest from the mind and practice of medicine today is the notion of "social engineering." This aversion to the practice of social medicine will, in the author's opinion, have to be overcome if the physician is to become an effective member of any suicide prevention program.

SOME GENERAL PROBLEMS IN THE IMPLEMENTATION OF SUICIDE PREVENTION PROGRAMS

The question arises, of course: What would happen if persons who are in a position to help were able to recognize the potential suicide as well as the potential suicide recognizes them? Would this necessarily infer that the suicidal person at last would have found the aid he so sorely sought? I think not. The position of the school districts and their personnel was made clear earlier in Chapter 2. They want no part of suicidal persons and the bad publicity that might rain upon them should they kill themselves. If these people were able to recognize a potential suicide, they would hasten to refer him to a doctor, a psychiatrist, a psychologist, a social worker—in fact, to any likely candidate outside of the school system. This leads one to wonder: What do these unlucky experts do?

In an article by Litman [4] concerned with the feelings of 200 psychotherapists toward patients who had recently committed suicide, and another article by Klugman et al.,[5] concerned with the problems of social workers, psychiatrists and psychologists and their suicidal patients, we find a common theme: fear, frustration, ambivalence and/or a "complete immobilization" on the part of the therapists toward their patients. The stress of the therapist-patient interaction "may induce problem reactions in the therapist. Among these are overwhelming effects such as anxiety, anger, or hopelessness, constriction of thought, impulsive actions, or complete immobilization." [6]

Why should these experts suffer "complete immobilization" or "anxiety?" After all, Klugman tells us that the extent of suicidal risk, which falls into one of three "broad categories" ("mild," "moderate," or "high"), is easy to evaluate, usually in one office visit. If the risk is "mild," "patients can be treated optimally at social work or family agencies." [7] These persons are presumably referred to a social worker or back to one for treatment. "High" risk patients, the article states, are best treated in psychiatric hospitals. It would seem that the therapists at the suicide prevention center (cited in the article) dealt primarily with "moderate risk" patients. Why all the anxiety on the part of experienced therapists with "moderate risk" patients, when "with help available and someone responding appropriately the suicide risk usually subsides within a short period of time." I believe the anxiety of the therapist stems from the fact that he is well aware that the suicidal risk of his patient, i.e., whether or not his patients really intend to kill themselves, is not easily or accurately assessed. What's more, even if it were true that the present crisis could be expected to subside with the appropriate intervention, what of the next crisis? Why did crisis situation "X" constitute grounds for suicide for this person and not someone else experiencing the same situation? What will have to happen in the future in order to reconstitute another "crisis?"

It is the lack of answers to these questions that causes anxiety, anger, or frustration in the therapist. I further believe that the answers to such questions are best sought in a process and not in any particular "crisis." More emphasis needs to be placed on reconstructing as well as possible the suicidal person's total biography and putting the "precipitating cause" into its proper context. Furthermore, I feel that the therapist ought to consider the accounts of his patients seriously. Granting that people do not always tell the truth or say what they mean, and that to accept everything at face value might prove misleading to the therapist, I feel it is more dangerous to go to the other extreme and not take the patients' accounts seriously. ". . . the rescuer should guard against basing his feelings and actions primarily on the content of the suicidal person's communications." [8] Clinicians are, of course, well aware of their shortcomings, and fear the suicide of their patient, an act which would reflect badly upon their reputation (or that of the agency). Then, too, there is the attack upon their ego, the responsibility and, should they fail, the guilt. In fact, the expert is subject to all of the woes of the non-expert and then some.

There is another aspect to the question of who would help if they were able. This is, at least in part, a question in the sociology of knowledge. To recognize someone's right to kill himself as stemming from his social situation is to recognize the necessity for social change. Professional persons who are presently sought out for assistance by potential suicides are usually "well situated." Such persons are not anxious for change and are in fact oriented toward maintaining the status quo. As such, they are obliged to rationalize the position of the potential suicide in such a way that a resolution in *his* problem cannot in any way be seen to entail a change in their own "life chances." One way to succeed in this is to postulate that the patient's problems are his personal problems stemming from a warped view of reality. Or, one might postulate an unconscious element so that the suicidal person's problems as he sees them are not his problems at all, but are only manifestations of the real problem of which he is unconscious. I believe that psychiatry's reluctance to take the accounts of patients seriously, as well as its aversion to the methods of milieu manipulation suggested by Meyer, is no accident. Nor is it an accident that they prefer a medical model. The convenience and "professionalism" of the medical model was quick to acquire new adherents. For example, the social workers of the 1920's and 1930's believed in social change as a means to individual change. Their contemporaries adhere to the reverse process,[9] notwithstanding the ideological rumblings in schools of social welfare to the contrary. The burden of responsibility is with the client or patient. Doctors no longer make house calls and social workers rarely go into the "field" to seek those requiring assistance. It is considered the responsibility of those who need help to seek it. Implicit in a client's seeking help is the clinician's assumption that this "motivation" will assist the clinician in "helping the client to help himself." Unfortunately, even among those who seek help a selective bias is at work. Not all who seek help find it. Potential suicides among low income, "non-verbal" or minority group persons are not considered by clinicians as desirable patients. Even among those therapists who are willing to help, the gap caused by class differences makes the establishment of a meaningful social relationship between patient and therapist a difficult task.

All of this points to the fact that there is more to the problem of suicide and its prevention than the recognition of the potential suicide. For example, many therapies specifically require that the therapist discourage the establishment of "personal" relationships. Such a therapeutic practice is particularly inappropriate in the case of suicidal patients. This problem is compounded by the clinician's inability to transcend his own model sufficiently to gain a better understanding of the position held by his patient who has not yet accepted the therapist's vocabulary of motives.

AN ORIENTATION TOWARD TREATMENT

One means of overcoming this problem within the setting of a suicide prevention center is to have former suicidal persons answering the phones instead of psychiatric social workers or other "trained" volunteers. The idea of a kind of "alcoholics anonymous" for suicidal persons is not new. At least one such service is currently in operation in London, England.[10]

Another possible approach might be the reinstatement of "moral treatment":

> Moral treatment demanded that the professional treater have deep personal commitment to the maintenance of the esteem and dignity of the patient, along with a rational and humanistic approach to human behavior. . . . All of these attitudes demanded by the moral treaters seem possible for social workers, who, like the originators of moral treatment, are non-medical practitioners. These concepts were operationalized in moral treatment by intimate, continuous, and frequent contact between the patient, the practitioner, and his family. The patient was welcome in the practitioner's home and office. The practitioner was fully familiar with the patient's life-style, wishes, aspirations, and past experiences. In short, the practitioner or moral treater became the patient's "significant other"—accepting, visible, ever accessible, and purposeful. While social workers, in general, are at least formally familiar with the patient's "social history," often through the hospital case record, the relationship between worker and patient today differs markedly from that prescribed by moral treatment. Today, patients are seen by appointment, usually at the worker's convenience and in the worker's office, where the formality of a desk and a procedure somehow structures or dominates the interactions. The patient may be seen only infrequently and formally. Patients do not enter the home or the private life of the worker, nor do they violate the worker's forty-hour week. To reach the worker, the patient must act through intermediaries; for example, receptionists, secretaries, and so on.[11]

CONCLUSIONS

The author's recommendations for the study of suicide as set forth in this book are based upon two considerations: first, a means of better understanding suicide, and secondly, the practical application of these findings to suicide prevention. By collecting case histories of suicides and suicide attempters and determining to what extent events in the lives of those individuals adhere to the formal aspects of the process previously outlined, I feel that a promising start could be made in this direction. The problem is not to be rid of suicide. As Durkheim realized, the cause of any social fact ought to be sought in prior social facts. The task as the author sees it, is to discover and alleviate those problems in the lives of suicidal individuals that have led away from meaningful social relationships. It was the individual's inability to establish and maintain such relationships, as a consequence of his circumstances, that led him to entertain and finally to attempt suicide in the first place. It is the author's opinion that if we wish to better understand suicide, in order to be able to anticipate and prevent it, we would do well to pick up where Durkheim prematurely left off and continue the search for its essential characteristics.

FOOTNOTES

1. Stengel *et al., op. cit.,* p. 17.

2. Dr. Matthew Ross, in an article entitled "Potential Suicides—What To Look For," *Journal of the American Medical Association,* CXCIV, No. 9 (November 29, 1965), 26.

3. Norman L. Farberow, "The Suicidal Patient and the Physician," *Mind,* I, No. 69 (March 1963), 69–75.

4. Robert E. Litman, "When Patients Commit Suicide," *American Journal of Psychotherapy,* XIX, No. 4 (1965), 570–76.

5. David J. Klugman *et al.,* "Suicide; Answering the Cry for Help," *Social Work,* X, No. 4 (October 1965), pp. 43–50.

6. *Ibid.,* p. 47.

7. *Ibid.,* p. 45.

8. *Ibid.*

9. Scott Briar, "The Casework Predicament," *Social Work,* XIII, No. 1 (January 1968), 7.

10. Louis I. Dublin, *Suicide: A Sociological and Statistical Study* (New York: Ronald Press Company, 1963), p. 182.

11. Dorothy Miller and Esther Blanc, "Concepts of 'Moral Treatment' for the Mentally Ill: Implications for Social Work with Posthospital Mental Patients," *The Social Service Review,* XXXXI, No. 1 (March 1967), 69–70. For a discussion of how these criticisms apply to psychiatrists in hospital settings, see: Merton J. Kahne, "Suicide among Patients in Mental Hospitals: A Study of the Psychiatrists Who Conducted Their Psychotherapy," *Psychiatry,* XXXI, No. 1 (February 1968), 32–43.

Bibliography

Bakwin, H. "Suicide in Children and Adolescents," *Journal of Pediatrics,* L (1957), 749–769.

Balser, B. and Masterton, J. "Suicide in Adolescents," *The American Journal of Psychiatry,* CXVI, No. 4 (1959), 400–407.

Beeley, A. L. "Juvenile Suicide: Some General Aspects of the Suicide Problem," *Social Service Review,* III (1929), 35–49.

Bender, Lauretta and Schilder, Paul. "Suicidal Preoccupations and Attempts in Children," *American Journal of Orthopsychiatry,* VII, No. 2 (1937), 225–234.

Bergstrand, C. G. and Otto, U. "Suicidal Attempts in Adolescence and Childhood," *Acta Pediatrica Espanola,* LI (1962), 17–26.

Binswanger, Ludwig. "The Case of Ellen West," in Rollo May *et al.* (eds.), *Existence.* New York: Basic Books, 1958.

Bond, Hubert. "Suicide from Sociological Aspect," *British Medical Journal,* II (1931), 234–239.

Bosselman, B. C. *Self Destruction: A Study of the Suicidal Impulse.* Springfield, Ill.: Charles A. Thomas, Publisher, 1958.

Briar, Scott. "The Casework Predicament," *Social Work,* XIII, No. 1 (1968), 5–11.

Cavan, Ruth S. *Suicide.* Chicago: University of Chicago Press, 1928.

Cressey, Donald R. *Other People's Money.* Glencoe, Ill.: Free Press, 1953.

Dorpat, Theodore L. *et al.* "Broken Homes and Attempted and Completed Suicide," *Archives of General Psychiatry,* XII (February 1965), 213–216.

Douglas, Jack D. *The Social Meanings of Suicide.* Princeton, New Jersey: Princeton University Press, 1967.

Durkheim, Emile. *Suicide: A Study in Sociology.* New York: Free Press, 1951.

Farberow, Norman L. "The Suicidal Patient and the Physician," *Mind,* I (March 1963), 69–75.

Farberow, Norman L. and Shneidman, E. *A Cry for Help.* New York: Blakiston, 1961.

Faretra, Gloria. "Depression in Teenagers." Among papers presented at a

Symposium on Depression, September 7, 1960. Detroit, Michigan: Michigan and Wayne County Academies of General Practice.

Firth, R. "Suicide and Risk-Taking in Tikopia Society." *Psychiatry* (February 1967), 1–18.

Gibbs, Jack P. and Martin, Walter T. "A Theory of Status Integration and Its Relationship to Suicide," *American Sociological Review,* XXIII, No. 2 (April 1958), 140–147.

————. *Status Integration and Suicide.* Eugene, Oregon: University of Oregon Press, 1964.

Goethe, Johann Wolfgang von. *The Sorrows of Young Werther.* New York: Rinehart and Co., 1958.

Greenwald, Harold. *The Call Girl.* New York: Ballantine Books, 1958.

Hartelius, H. "Suicide in Sweden 1925–1950," *Acta Psychiat. Scand.,* XXXII (1957), 151–181.

Henry, Andrew F. and Short, James F. *Suicide and Homicide.* Glencoe, Ill.: The Free Press, 1954.

Hume, David. "Of Suicide," in *Hume's Ethical Writings.* Edited by Alasdair MacIntyre. New York: Collier Books, 1965.

Iga, Mamoru. "Suicides of Japanese Youths," *Sociology and Social Research,* XLVI, No. 1 (October 1961), 75–90.

Jacobziner, Harold. "Attempted Suicides in Adolescence," *The Journal of the American Medical Association,* CXCI (January 4, 1965), 7–11.

Jacobs, Jerry. "A Phenomenological Study of Suicide Notes," *Social Problems,* XV, No. 1 (Summer 1967), 60–72.

————. "The Use of Religion in Constructing the Moral Justification of Suicide," in *Deviance and Respectability: The Social Construction of Moral Meanings,* edited by Jack Douglas, Basic Books, 1970.

Jacobs, Jerry and Teicher, Joseph D. "Broken Homes and Social Isolation in Attempted Suicide," *International Journal of Social Psychiatry,* Vol. XIII, No. 2, 1967, pp. 139–149.

Jan-Tausch, James. "Suicides of Children 1960–1963, New Jersey Public School Studies," bulletin put out by State of New Jersey, Department of Education.

Kahne, Merton J. "Suicide Among Patients in Mental Hospitals: A Study of the Psychiatrists Who Conducted Their Psychotherapy," *Psychiatry,* XXXI, No. 1 (February 1968), 32–43.

————. "Suicide Research: A Critical Review of Strategies and Potentialities in Mental Hospitals," *The International Journal of Social Psychiatry,* XII, No. 2 (Spring 1966), 120–129.

Klugman, David J. *et al.* "Suicide: Answering the Cry for Help," *Social Work,* X, No. 4 (October 1965), 43–50.

Kobler, Arthur L. and Scotland, Ezra. *The End of Hope*. Glencoe, Ill., The Free Press, 1964.

Lendrum, F. C. "A Thousand Cases of Attempted Suicide," *American Journal of Psychiatry*, XC (1933), 479–500.

Lidz, Theodore. "Adolph Meyer and the Development of American Psychiatry," *American Journal of Psychiatry*, CXXIII, No. 3 (September 1966), 320–332.

Litman, Robert E. *et al.* "Investigations of Equivocal Suicides," *The Journal of the American Medical Association*, CXXCIV (June 22, 1963), 924–929.

Litman, Robert E. "When Patients Commit Suicide," *American Journal of Psychotherapy*, XIX, No. 4 (1965), 570–576.

———. In an article entitled "Potential Suicides—What to Look For," *The Journal of the American Medical Association*, CXCIV, No. 9 (November 29, 1965), 27.

Mason, Percy. "Suicide in Adolescents," *Psychoanalytic Review*, XLI, (1954), 48–54.

Meerloo, J. A. M. *Suicide and Mass Suicide*. New York: Grune and Stratton, Inc., 1962.

Miller, Dorothy and Blanc, Esther. "Concepts of 'Moral Treatment' for the Mentally Ill: Implications for Social Work with Post-Hospital Mental Patients," *The Social Service Review*, XXXXI, No. 1 (March 1967), 66–74.

Mills, C. Wright. "Situated Actions and Vocabularies of Motive," *American Sociological Review*, V, No. 6 (December 1940), 904–913.

Miner, J. R. "Suicide and Its Relation to Climatic and Other Factors," *American Journal of Hygiene*, Monographic Series No. 2 (November 2, 1922), 72–112.

Morselli, E. A. *Suicide: An Essay on Comparative Moral Statistics*. New York: D. Appleton and Co., 1889.

Offer, D. and Barglow, P. "Adolescent and Young Adult Self-Mutilation Incidents in a General Psychiatric Hospital," *Archives of General Psychiatry*, III (1960), 194–204.

Parnell, R. W. and Skottowe, I. "Toward Preventing Suicide," *Lancet*, I (1957), 206–208.

Porkony, Alex D. "A Follow Up Study of 618 Suicidal Patients," *The American Journal of Psychiatry*, CXXII, No. 10 (1966), 1109–1116.

Porterfield, A. L. "Suicide and Crime in the Social Structure of an Urban Setting: Fort Worth 1930–1950," *American Sociological Review*, XVII (1952), 341–343.

Powell, Elwin H. "Occupational Status and Suicide: Toward a Redefinition of Anomie," *American Sociological Review*, XXIII (April 1950), 131–139.

Robins, Eli *et al.* "The Communication of Suicidal Intent: A Study of 134 Consecutive Cases of Successful (Completed) Suicide," *The American Journal of Psychiatry*, CXV, No. 8 (February 1959), 724–733.

Robins, Eli. In an article entitled "Potential Suicides—What to Look For," *The Journal of the American Medical Association*, CXCIV, No. 9 (November 29, 1965), 27.

Rosen, A. "Detection of Suicidal Patients: An Example of Some Limitations in the Prediction of Infrequent Events," *Journal of Consulting Psychology*, XVIII (1954), 397–403.

Sainsbury, Peter. *Suicide in London*. London: Chapman and Hall, Ltd., 1955.

Schechter, Marshall D. "The Recognition and Treatment of Suicide in Children," in *Clues to Suicide*. Edited by Edwin Shneidman and Norman Farberow. New York: McGraw-Hill Book Co., Inc., 1957.

Schneer, Henry I. *et al.* "Events and Conscious Ideation Leading to Suicidal Behavior in Adolescence," *Psychiatry Quarterly*, XXXV (1961), 507–515.

Schrut, Albert. "Suicidal Adolescents and Children," *The Journal of the American Medical Association*, CXXCVIII (June 29, 1964), 1103–1107.

Schutz, Alfred. *Collected Papers*, Vol. I: *The Problem of Social Reality*. The Hague: Martinus Nijhoff, 1962.

Shneidman, Edwin S. and Farberow, Norman L. Appendix: "Genuine and Simulated Suicide Notes," in *Clues to Suicide*. New York: McGraw-Hill Book Co., Inc., 1957.

————. "TAT Heroes of Suicidal and Non-Suicidal Subjects," *Journal of Projective Techniques*, XXII (1958), 211–288.

Sifneos, P. *et al.* "Preliminary Psychiatric Study of Attempted Suicide," *The American Journal of Psychiatry*, CXII (1956), 882–888.

Stearns, Warren A. "Cases of Probable Suicide in Young Persons Without Obvious Motivation," *The Journal of the Maine Medical Association*, XLIV (1953), 16–23.

Stengel, E. and Cook, Nancy. *Attempted Suicide*. London: Chapman and Hall, Ltd., 1958.

Stone, A. A. "A Syndrome of Serious Suicidal Intent," *Archives of General Psychiatry*, III (1960), 331–339.

Swanson, David W. "Suicide in Identical Twins," *The American Journal of Psychiatry*, CXVI (1960), 934–941.

Tabachnick, Norman. "Observations on Attempted Suicide," *Clues to Suicide*. New York: McGraw-Hill Book Co., Inc. (1957), 164–169.

Teicher, Joseph D. and Jacobs, Jerry. "Adolescents Who Attempt Suicide: Preliminary Findings," *The American Journal of Psychiatry*, CXXII, No. 11 (May 1966), 1248–1257.

Toolan, J. M. "Depression in Children and Adolescents," *American Journal of Orthopsychiatry*, XXXII (1962), 404–415.

———. "Suicide and Suicidal Attempts in Children and Adolescents," *The American Journal of Psychiatry*, CXVIII (1962), 719–724.

Tuckman, Jacob *et al.* "Emotional Content of Suicide Notes," *The American Journal of Psychiatry*, CXVI (July 1959), 59–63.

———. "Credibility of Suicide Notes," *The American Journal of Psychiatry*, CXVI (1960), 1104.

Tuckman, J. and Connon, H. E. "Attempted Suicide in Adolescents," *The American Journal of Psychiatry*, CXIX (1962), 228–232.

Wahl, Charles W. "Suicide as a Magical Act," in *Clues to Suicide*, edited by Edwin Shneidman and Norman Farberow. New York: McGraw-Hill Book Co., Inc., 1957.

West, D. J. *Murders Followed by Suicide.* London: Heinemann Educational Books, Ltd., Morrison and Gibb, Ltd., 1965.

Wolfgang, M. E. "Suicide by Means of Victim-Precipitated Homicide," *Journal of Clinical and Experimental Psychopathology and Quarterly Review of Psychiatry and Neurology*, XX (1959), 335–349.

Appendix

Table A

Description of Matched Pairs

| | 31 Matched Pairs | | | | | | | | 19 Non-Matched Experimental Adolescents | | | | |
	Controls				Experimentals								
Case No.	Age	Race	Sex	Mother's Education	Mother's Education	Sex	Race	Age	Case No.	Age	Race	Sex	Mother's Education
1	15	W	F	4	4	F	W	15	32	14	W	F	1
2	15	W	F	1	1	F	W	15	33	14	W	F	2
3	15	W	F	2	2	F	W	15	34	14	W	F	1
4	16	W	F	1	1	F	W	16	35	16	W	F	3
5	16	W	F	1	1	F	W	15	36	15	W	F	1
6	16	W	F	2	2	F	W	16	37	15	W	F	2
7	16	W	F	0	0	F	W	16	38	15	W	F	2
8	17	W	F	2	2	F	W	17	39	17	W	F	2
9	17	W	F	1	1	F	W	17	40	17	W	F	3
10	17	W	F	1	1	F	W	18	41	18	W	F	1
11	14	M	F	1	1	F	M	14	42	14	M	F	1
12	15	M	F	3	2	F	M	14	43	16	M	F	0
13	15	M	F	1	1	F	M	15	44	15	M	F	0
14	15	M	F	1	1	F	M	16	45	14	N	F	0
15	16	M	F	2	2	F	M	16	46	14	N	F	2
16	18	M	F	1	1	F	M	17	47	14	N	F	2
17	18	M	F	0	0	F	M	16	48	16	W	M	1
18	15	N	F	1	2	F	N	15	49	17	M	M	0
19	16	N	F	1	3	F	N	16	50	18	M	M	2
20	16	N	F	1	1	F	N	17					
21	17	N	F	2	2	F	N	15					
22	17	N	F	4	4	F	N	18					
23	17	W	M	2	2	M	W	15					
24	17	W	M	2	2	M	W	14					
25	17	W	M	4	1	M	W	15					
26	18	W	M	2	1	M	W	16					
27	16	M	M	1	1	M	M	16					
28	17	M	M	1	1	M	M	17					
29	14	N	M	1	1	M	N	14					
30	15	N	M	1	1	M	N	16					
31	15	N	M	1	1	M	N	18					

Mother's Education: 0 = No information; 1 = Not a high school graduate; 2 = High school graduate only; 3 = Some college; 4 = College graduate.

Table B

Total Scores for Selected Events in the Life Histories of Experimental and Control Adolescents of the Matched and Non-Matched Sets

	Number of Residence Moves		Number of School Changes, Left Back 1 Semester or More		Suspended for Reasons Other than Scholarship		Not Enrolled when Interviewed	
	Exp.	Cont.	Exp.	Cont.	Exp.	Cont.	Exp.	Cont.
31 Matched Pairs								
Birth to 1959:								
Total Occurrences	76	77	37	30				
Total Persons Involved	27	24	21	14				
1959 to Interview:								
Total Occurrences	74	45	62	28	2	1	10	
Total Persons Involved	28	17	24	16	2	1	10	
19 Non-Matched Pairs								
Birth to 1959:								
Total Occurrences	63		29					
Total Persons Involved	17		14					
1959 to Interview:								
Total Occurrences	59		44		9		6	
Total Persons Involved	16		17		5		6	

Table B (*Continued*)

Serious Romance Prior to Interview		Romance Broken up or Threat of Break-up		Pregnant or Thought So from Romance		Institution-alization of S/A or Family Member (Juvenile Hall, etc.)		Serious Physical Illness of Adolescent or Injury		Number of Hospitali-zations for Adolescent		Serious Physical Illness of Other Family Member	
Exp.	Cont.	Exp.	Cont.	Exp.	Cont.	Exp.	Cont.	Exp.	Cont.	Exp.	Cont.	Exp.	Cont.
						1		16	8	5	1	6	
						1		9	7	5	1	6	
13	7	8		3		10	1	14	5	12	3	6	4
13	7	8		3		6	1	13	5	8	2	5	4
						3		4				4	
						1		4				4	
8		6		5		8		2		7		2	
8		6		5		4		2		6		1	

Table B (*Continued*)

	Number of Hospitalizations for Other Family Members		Parents Separated or Divorced Number of Times		Living with Relative (Parent Not There) Number of Times		Parent Remarried: Step or Common Law Enter Family Number of Times	
	Exp.	Cont.	Exp.	Cont.	Exp.	Cont.	Exp.	Cont.
31 Matched Pairs								
Birth to 1959:								
Total Occurrences	6		14	7	4	2	8	4
Total Persons Involved	4		12	7	4	2	5	4
1959 to Interview:								
Total Occurrences	11	4	19	3	13	2	10	1
Total Persons Involved	8	4	14	2	9	2	9	1
19 Non-Matched Pairs								
Birth to 1959:								
Total Occurrences	4		18		5		7	
Total Persons Involved	4		12		5		4	
1959 to Interview:								
Total Occurrences	2		12		10		7	
Total Persons Involved	2		9		7		6	

Table B (*Continued*)

Both (1 when only 1 Parent) Parents Working		Heavy Drinking a Family Problem		Death of Family Member or Close Friend		Number of S/A by Parents		Number of S/A by Friends or Other Relatives		Prior S/A's by Adolescent: Number	
Exp.	Cont.	Exp.	Cont.	Exp.	Cont.	Exp.	Cont.	Exp.	Cont.	Exp.	Cont.
10	7	5	4	4	3	2				1	
10	7	5	4	3	3	2				1	
20	19	6	1	6	2	10		10		20	
20	19	6	1	5	2	3		8		13	
6		4		1		4		1			
6		4		1		2		1			
12		3		7		3		10		22	
12		3		5		3		7		10	

Table C

Events in the Lives of Experimental and Control Adolescents from Birth through 1958

Column headers (each measure has Exp. and Cont. subcolumns):

- Number of Residence Moves
- Number of School Changes; Left Back 1 Semester or More
- Institutionalization of Adolescent or Family Member
- Serious Physical Illness of Adolescent or Injury
- Number of Hospitalizations of Adolescent
- Serious Physical Illness in Other Family Member
- Number of Hospitalizations of Other Family Member
- Parents Separated or Divorced Number of Times

Case Number	Residence Moves Exp	Cont	School Changes Exp	Cont	Institution. Exp	Cont	Ser. Phys. Ill. Adol. Exp	Cont	Num. Hosp. Adol. Exp	Cont	Ser. Phys. Ill. Other Fam. Exp	Cont	Num. Hosp. Other Fam. Exp	Cont	Parents Sep./Div. Exp	Cont
Females																
1.	4						1									
2.	2		1												1	
3.	3	3	3	2			1	1	1	1	1					
4.	8	1	2		1								3			
5.	1	2	1	1											1	
6.	6	3	4	1											1	
7.	1	7	1	7			2									1
8.	4		1						1							
9.	4	4	2	3											3	1
10.	1		1				2									
11.	2	3	2													
12.		6		1											1	
13.	2	6		2												1
14.	2	4	1	2									1		1	
15.	1	2		1												1
16.		5		3			1		1		1					1
17.	5			3			1								1	
18.	3	5					1	1	1							
19.	3	1	1	1							1					
20.	2	1	2													
21.	3	1	1												1	
22.	3		3								1		1			
Males																
23.	1	1	2				1				1				1	
24.	2	1		1												
25.		1							1		1		1		1	
26.	3		1							1						
27.	6	7	2	3						1						1
28.		3		2			1		1							
29.	1	5					1	1							1	1
30.	2	3	2										1			
31.	2	2	1													
Total Number of Occurrences	76	77	37	30	1	0	16	8	5	1	6	0	6	0	14	7
Total Persons Involved	27	24	21	14	1	0	9	7	5	1	6	0	4	0	12	7

Table C (*Continued*)

Group	Case Number	Living with Relative; Number of Times (Parent Not There)		Parent Remarries; Stepparent Enters Family		Parents (1 when only 1) Working		Drinking a Family Problem		Death of Family Member or Close Friend		Number of S/A by Parents		Number of S/A by Friends or Other Relatives		Prior S/A's by Adolescent: Number	
		Exp.	Cont.	Exp.	Cont.	Exp.	Cont.	Exp.	Cont.	Exp.	Cont.	Exp.	Cont.	Exp.	Cont.	Exp.	Cont.
Females	1.						1										
	2.	1				1		1			1						
	3.		1														
	4.	1															
	5.								1								
	6.			2					1	2							
	7.		1		1												
	8.							1				1					
	9.			3				1		1							
	10.																
	11.																
	12.					1	1										
	13.																
	14.					1	1										
	15.				1		1										
	16.				1						1					1	
	17.			1		1											
	18.				1		1										
	19.											1					
	20.																
	21.	1				1	1										
	22.						1		1								
Males	23.			1		1											
	24.																
	25.							1									
	26.			1		1				1							
	27.							1	1								
	28.					1											
	29.	1				1											
	30.					1					1						
	31.																
Total Number of Occurrences		4	2	8	4	10	7	5	4	4	3	2	0	0	0	1	0
Total Persons Involved		4	2	5	4	10	7	5	4	3	3	2	0	0	0	1	0

Table D

Events in the Lives of Experimental and Control Adolescents from 1959 to Interview

Case Number	Number of Residential Moves from 1959 on Exp.	Cont.	Number of School Changes; Left Back 1 Semester or More (1959 on) Exp.	Cont.	Suspended for Reasons Other than Scholarship Exp.	Cont.	Not Enrolled when Interviewed Exp.	Cont.	Serious Romance Prior to Interview Exp.	Cont.
Females										
1.	2						1			
2.	4		3						1	1
3.	1	1	1							
4.	1	1	7	1			1			1
5.	7	3	7	3			1			
6.	3		2							
7.	3	7	3	7					1	
8.	1								1	
9.	4	3	2	1			1		1	
10.	2				1					
11.	3	2	3	1						
12.	3	2	1	1					1	
13.	3	3	2	1						
14.	1	4	1	3					1	
15.		3		1						1
16.		1	1	1			1			
17.	1	2	1	1						
18.	3	3	2	1		1	1			
19.	2		3		1					1
20.	2		2				1		1	
21.	1									
22.							1		1	
Males										
23.	5	1	5	1			1			1
24.	4		3							
25.	1		1							
26.	2		2						1	
27.	4	1	3				1			
28.	2								1	1
29.	2		2	1						
30.	5	7	3	2					1	
31.	2	1	2	2			1		1	1
Total No. of Occurrences	74	45	62	28	2	1	10	0	13	7
Total Persons Involved	28	17	24	16	2	1	10	0	13	7

Table D (*Continued*)

Romance Broken up or Threat of Break-up		Pregnant or Thought So from Romance		Institution-alization of S/A or Family Member (Juvenile Hall, etc.)		Serious Physical Illness of Adolescent or Injury		Number of Hospitali-zations for Adolescent		Serious Physical Illness of Other Family Member	
Exp.	Cont.	Exp.	Cont.	Exp.	Cont.	Exp.	Cont.	Exp.	Cont.	Exp.	Cont.
				1		1	1				
				1							
						1				1	
						1				1	
1		1									
						1	1		2		
1		1				1		1			
1											
1										1	
								1		2	1
							1				
1		1									
						2					
						1		1			
						1					
						1					
											1
1											
							1				
						1		1			
				2		1		5			
				1	1	1	1	1	1	1	
								1			
					1			1			1
1				2							
						1					
1				1							1
				3							
8	0	3	0	10	1	14	5	12	3	6	4
8	0	3	0	6	1	13	5	8	2	5	4

Table D (*Continued*)

Case Number	Number of Hospitalizations for Other Family Member		Parents Separated or Divorced Number of Times		Living with Relative (Parent Not There) Number of Times		Parent Remarried; Step or Common Law Enter Family No. of Times	
	Exp.	Cont.	Exp.	Cont.	Exp.	Cont.	Exp.	Cont.
Females								
1.			1					
2.					3		1	
3.								
4.	1		1		2		1	
5.	1		2		1		2	
6.							1	
7.			1			1	1	
8.	1		1					
9.							1	
10.	2				1			
11.	1		1					
12.					1			
13.								
14.			1					
15.								
16.			2					
17.					1	1		
18.	1		1					
19.		1						
20.								
21.			1		1		1	
22.	3	1						
Males								
23.			2				1	
24.			2		1			
25.	1							
26.			1					
27.		1	2	2				
28.								
29.					2		1	
30.		1						1
31.				1				
Total No. of Occurrences	11	4	19	3	13	2	10	1
Total Persons Involved	8	4	14	2	9	2	9	1

Table D (*Continued*)

Both (1 when only 1 Parent) Parents Working		Heavy Drinking a Family Problem		Death of Family Member or Close Friend		Number of S/A by Parents		Number of S/A by Friends or Other Relatives		Prior S/A's by Adolescent:
Exp.	Cont.	Exp.	Cont.	Exp.	Cont.	Exp.	Cont.	Exp.	Cont.	Number
	1			2						
1										1
1		1				6				
1	1									2
1	1									2
1	1	1						1		1
					1			2		1
1								1		1
1	1							1		1
1										
1	1	1								
	1	1						2		
1	1							1		3
				1				1		1
	1									
1	1									
1	1									
1	1									
	1				1	3				
1	1									
1										4
1	1			1						1
1		1								
	1	1	1			1		1		1
1	1			1						
1	1			1						
	1									1
1										
20	19	6	1	6	2	10	0	10	0	20	0
20	19	6	1	5	2	3	0	8	0	13	0

Table E

Events in the Lives of Nineteen Unmatched S/A from 1959 to the Time of the Interview and from Birth to 1959

	Case Number	Number of Residential Moves		Number of School Changes; Left Back 1 Semester or More		Suspended for Reasons Other than Scholarship		Not Enrolled when Interviewed		Serious Romance Prior to Interview	
		1959 on	Prior to 1959	1959 on	Prior to 1959	1959 on	Prior to 1959	1959 on	Prior to 1959	1959 on	Prior to 1959
		Experimentals————————————————————————————→									
Females	32.	7	4	5	1					1	
	33.	7	6	7	4						
	34.	5	6	5	1					1	
	35.	4	2	4	2			1			
	36.	4	5	2							
	37.	3	3	5	2	1					
	38.		2	1	1					1	
	39.	2	5	1	3						
	40.		4	1	3						
	41.		1	1				1		1	
	42.	4		2				1			
	43.	6	2	2	1					1	
	44.	3	1		1	1		1			
	45.	1		1							
	46.	2	6	2	3					1	
	47.	2	4	1	2	1		1			
Males	48.	5	4	2		5					
	49.	3	3	2	3	1		1		1	
	50.	1	5		2					1	
	Total Number of Occurrences	59	63	44	29	9	0	6	0	8	0
	Total Persons Involved	16	17	17	14	5	0	6	0	8	0

Romance Broken up or Threat of Break-up		Pregnant or Thought So from Romance		Institutionalization of S/A or Family Member (Juvenile Hall, etc.)		Serious Physical Illness of Adolescent or Injury		Number of Hospitalizations for Adolescent		Serious Physical Illness of Other Family Member	
1959 on	Prior to 1959	1959 on	Prior to 1959	1959 on	Prior to 1959	1959 on	Prior to 1959	1959 on	Prior to 1959	1959 on	Prior to 1959
											1
								1			
1								2			
								1			1
		1									
1		1									
						1					
1							1	1			
					3						1
1		1		1				1			
				3			1				1
		1									
		1		1				1			
							1			2	
1				3		1					
1							1				
6	0	5	0	8	3	2	4	7	0	2	4
6	0	5	0	4	1	2	4	6	0	1	4

Table E (*Continued*)

	Case Number	Number of Hospitalizations for Other Family Member		Parents Separated or Divorced Number of Times		Living with Relative (Parent Not There) Number of Times		Parent Remarried; Step or Common Law Enter Family No. of Times	
		1959 on	Prior to 1959	1959 on	Prior to 1959	1959 on	Prior to 1959	1959 on	Prior to 1959
Females	32.		1	3		1		2	
	33.			1	2				1
	34.						1		
	35.	1	1						
	36.			2	2	1	1		2
	37.			1	1			1	
	38.			1	3			1	3
	39.			1					
	40.				1				
	41.								
	42.				1				
	43.				1	4	1		
	44.		1		1	1	1		
	45.				1				
	46.			1		1			
	47.			1	1	1	1	1	1
Males	48.	1		1					
	49.		1		1	1		1	
	50.				3			1	
	Total Number of Occurrences	2	4	12	18	10	5	7	7
	Total Persons Involved	2	4	9	12	7	5	6	4

Table E (*Continued*)

← ———— Experimentals

Both (1 when only 1 Parent) Parents Working		Heavy Drinking a Family Problem		Death of Family Member or Close Friend		Number of S/A by Parents		Number of S/A by Friends or Other Relatives		Prior S/A's by Adolescent: Number	
1959 on	Prior to 1959	1959 on	Prior to 1959	1959 on	Prior to 1959	1959 on	Prior to 1959	1959 on	Prior to 1959	1959 on	Prior to 1959
1						1		2		1	
1	1	1						1		1	
1											
1				1				2		5	
1			1	2		1		2			
1				1				1		1	
				2				1			
							2				
1	1	1			1					1	
	1		1						1	1	
	1	1		1				1		3	
	1		1							3	
1	1										
							2			4	
1										2	
1						1					
1											
1			1								
12	6	3	4	7	1	3	4	10	1	22	0
12	6	3	4	5	1	3	2	7	1	10	0

Table F

Rank Order of Number of Behavioral Problems Which Originated Within the Last Five Years

Using Mann-Whitney U Test, reject null hypothesis at .001 level. Experimental and Control combined. Experimental—N=50; Control—N=31; Total N=81.

Rank	No. of Problems	Group	Sex	Age	Rank	No. of Problems	Group	Sex	Age
1	14	C	F	17	41	4	E	F	14
2	12	E	M	18	42	4	C	M	14
3	12	E	F	16	43	4	C	F	17
4	11	E	F	14	44	4	E	F	17
5	10	E	F	17	45	4	C	M	17
6	10	E	F	16	46	4	E	F	16
7	10	E	F	15	47	4	C	F	15
8	10	E	M	17	48	3	C	F	16
9	9	E	F	15	49	3	E	F	15
10	9	E	M	16	50	3	E	F	18
11	9	E	F	15	51	3	C	F	15
12	9	E	F	15	52	3	C	M	15
13	9	E	M	18	53	3	E	F	16
14	8	C	F	15	54	3	E	F	17
15	8	E	F	16	55	3	C	F	18
16	8	E	F	17	56	3	C	M	18
17	8	C	F	14	57	3	E	F	15
18	8	E	F	17	58	3	C	F	17
19	7	E	F	14	59	3	C	M	17
20	7	E	M	16	60	3	C	F	17
21	7	E	F	15	61	3	E	F	18
22	7	E	F	14	62	3	C	M	15
23	7	E	F	16	63	3	E	M	17
24	6	E	F	14	64	3	C	F	16
25	6	E	F	16	65	3	C	M	17
26	6	E	F	14	66	2	E	F	15
27	6	E	F	17	67	2	C	F	16
28	6	E	F	15	68	2	C	F	15
29	6	E	M	16	69	2	E	M	15
30	6	E	F	16	70	2	E	F	16
31	5	C	M	16	71	2	C	F	15
32	5	E	F	15	72	2	E	F	16
33	5	C	M	17	73	1	C	M	15
34	5	E	F	15	74	1	C	F	15
35	5	E	M	14	75	1	C	F	16
36	5	E	M	16	76	1	C	F	16
37	5	E	F	14	77	1	C	F	15
38	4	E	F	14	78	1	C	F	16
39	4	E	F	18	79	1	C	F	16
40	4	C	F	17	80	0	C	F	18
					81	0	E	M	15

Table G

Rank Order of Number of Disciplinary Techniques Used by Mothers of Experimental and Control Groups

Using Mann-Whitney U Test, reject null hypothesis at .01 level.
(Experimental: N=49; Control—N=32)

Rank	No. of Disciplines	Group	Sex	Age	Rank	No. of Disciplines	Group	Sex	Age
1	9	E	F	15	41	4	E	F	14
2	8	E	F	15	42	4	C	F	18
3	8	E	F	15	43	4	C	M	16
4	8	E	F	14	44	4	C	M	15
5	8	E	M	16	45	4	E	M	18
6	7	E	F	16	46	3	C	F	15
7	7	E	M	15	47	3	C	F	16
8	7	E	F	18	48	3	E	F	16
9	7	E	M	14	49	3	C	F	18
10	7	E	F	16	50	3	E	F	16
11	7	E	F	15	51	3	C	M	15
12	7	C	M	17	52	3	C	F	15
13	7	C	F	15	53	3	C	F	15
14	7	C	F	17	54	3	E	F	15
15	7	E	M	17	55	2	C	M	17
16	6	E	F	16	56	2	E	F	15
17	6	C	M	17	57	2	E	F	18
18	6	E	M	16	58	2	E	F	14
19	6	E	F	14	59	2	C	M	18
20	6	E	F	15	60	2	C	F	14
21	6	E	F	15	61	2	C	F	16
22	6	E	F	16	62	2	C	F	15
23	6	E	F	17	63	2	C	F	17
24	6	E	M	16	64	2	E	F	15
25	5	E	F	17	65	2	E	M	15
26	5	E	F	14	66	2	C	F	15
27	5	E	F	15	67	2	E	F	14
28	5	E	M	16	68	2	E	F	17
29	5	E	F	14	69	2	E	F	16
30	5	E	M	18	70	2	C	F	15
31	5	E	F	16	71	2	C	F	16
32	5	E	F	15	72	2	C	M	15
33	5	C	M	14	73	2	C	M	17
34	5	C	F	16	74	1	C	F	17
35	5	C	F	17	75	1	C	F	17
36	5	C	F	16	76	1	C	F	16
37	5	E	F	16	77	1	E	M	17
38	4	C	F	16	78	1	E	F	18
39	4	E	F	17	79	1	E	F	17
40	4	E	F	17	80	1	E	F	16
					81	1	E	F	14

Table H

Per Cent of Experimental and Control Parents Using Selected Disciplinary Techniques (as Perceived by the Adolescent)

	Matched Pairs			
	Experimental Mothers (N=30)		Control Mothers (N=31)	
1. Whipping	33%	(10)	18%	(6)
2. Spanking (slapping)	50%	(15)	37%	(12)
3. Withholding privileges	67%	(20)	65%	(21)
4. Withholding approval or affection	20%	(6)	6%	(2)
5. Holding out promises of rewards	20%	(6)	31%	(10)
6. Talking things over, discussing the problem	67%	(20)	75%	(24)
7. Criticizing	63%	(19)	28%	(9)
8. Nagging	63%	(19)	25%	(8)
9. Yelling	77%	(23)	34%	(11)
10. Other (sent to bed without dinner, etc.)	3%	(1)	3%	(1)

Table H (*Continued*)

				Non-Matched Pairs			
Experimental Fathers (N=23)		Control Fathers (N=25)		Experimental Mothers (N=19)		Experimental Fathers (N=19)	
39%	(9)	32%	(8)	42%	(8)	60%	(12)
43%	(10)	40%	(10)	47%	(9)	53%	(10)
43%	(10)	52%	(13)	68%	(13)	47%	(9)
13%	(3)	8%	(2)	21%	(4)	21%	(4)
17%	(4)	32%	(8)	26%	(5)	15%	(3)
35%	(8)	40%	(10)	53%	(10)	31%	(6)
39%	(9)	28%	(7)	60%	(12)	31%	(6)
26%	(6)	12%	(3)	58%	(11)	21%	(4)
60%	(14)	20%	(5)	79%	(15)	47%	(9)
4%	(1)	4%	(1)	15%	(3)	5%	(1)

Table I

Composite Picture of the Distribution of Selected Events in the Life of the Adolescents Comprising the 31 Matched Pairs

	Matched Pairs						
	Experimental (N=31)						
	Prior S/A's by Adolescent	S/A by Parents	Serious Physical Illness in Adolescent	Parents Remarry or (Common Law)	Separation or Divorce of Parents	Number of School Changes	Number of Residential Changes
1947							
	0	1	2	1	3	0	12
	0	0	6	1	2	0	17
1953							
	0	0	2	2	6	16	21
	1	1	6	4	0	23	26
1959							
	4	1	3	9	11	35	42
	16	9	11	1	8	26	32
1964–65							

Table I (*Continued*)

	Matched Pairs						
	Control (N=31)						
Number of Residential Changes	Number of School Changes	Separation or Divorce of Parents	Parents Remarry or (Common Law)	Serious Physical Illness, Injury in Adolescent	S/A by Parents	Prior S/A's by Adolescent	
							1947
7	0	1	1	3	0	0	
17	0	0	0	2	0	0	
							1953
33	11	5	1	2	0	0	
19	17	2	2	1	0	0	
							1959
25	19	0	1	3	0	0	
20	8	2	0	2	0	0	
							1964–65

Author Index

Subject Index